MANAGING THE MULTINATIONALS

Managing
the Multinationals
Preparing for Tomorrow

by BUSINESS INTERNATIONAL S.A.
in conjunction with the
Centre d'Études Industrielles, Geneva

London · George Allen & Unwin Ltd
RUSKIN HOUSE   MUSEUM STREET

First published in 1972

© George Allen & Unwin Ltd, 1972
ISBN 0 04 658131 6

Printed in Great Britain
in 10 point Times Roman type
by Alden & Mowbray Ltd
at the Alden Press, Oxford

FOREWORD

This book has been inspired by the First European Management Symposium, held in Davos, Switzerland, on the occasion of the twenty-fifth anniversary of the Centre d'Études Industrielles (CEI), a centre for education in international management. The theme of the symposium was 'Preparing for Tomorrow – Management Plans for Action'. A number of dramatic events have since transpired, such as the successful conclusion of negotiations for prospective entry of Great Britain into the Common Market, the announcement of the proposed visit of the President of the United States to China, and a virtual breakdown of the world monetary system in effect since the Bretton Woods Conference in 1944. All the above events and many others yet to come will have a significant impact on business firms. They confirm, therefore, the validity of the symposium and of this book, whose objectives are to help managers cope more effectively with the changing environment.

This book has a number of distinguishing features: it deals with the environmental changes in very specific terms; it makes a series of bold predictions about changes to come, presenting in each case a single picture rather than alternative scenarios; it offers some very specific action recommendations. There is, of course, no certainty about specific happenings, but the directions of change are much more visible. The intention is to increase the concern for and the ability to cope with change, among other things through more systematic strategy formulation, better use of information technology, wise internationalization and better development of managerial resources.

The symposium and this book play complementary roles of education and information, both aimed at improved management in an international context. The symposium was an educational event. The CEI designed the programme and provided much of the talent from the academic and business circles that carried the event forward. It was a fitting task for the oldest international management school. The presence of several hundred senior executives in Davos, just like the annual flow of hundreds of executives through the CEI's distinctive international programme in Geneva, indicate an acceptance of its mission, viz. to provide continuous education opportunities for internationally-minded managers.

The book is the product of Business International whose editors and writers are professional interpreters of the moving global scene. The organization was established eighteen years ago to serve multinational firms by continuously supplying them with evaluated information about the international environment in which they must function. It also drew upon the resources of Dr Klaus Schwab, who was responsible for the First European Management Symposium.

Peter Drucker has written that 'Knowledge, during the last few decades, has become the central capital, the cost center, and the crucial resource of the economy.' The aim of both the Davos Symposium and the book based on it is to contribute to management's knowledge of the international business environment and the techniques for coping with it effectively.

BOHDAN HAWRYLYSHYN

September 6, 1971   *Director, Centre d'Études Industrielle*

CONTENTS

GENERAL INTRODUCTION

This study is divided into two sections. The first section forecasts some of the more consequential environmental opportunities and challenges that corporations will face in the next decade.

At the First European Management Symposium in Davos, in 1971, on whose deliberations this work is based, Dr Herman Kahn, Director of the Hudson Institute, defined his own view of these challenges in a statement which highlighted the expanding role of the Japanese economy and reaffirmed the built-in momentum of contemporary technology, in the following words:

> I am willing to make a prediction rather than a projection that the rise of Japan in 1970 will be looked on by many people as the historical event of this century and that the next thirty, or forty, or fifty years is going to be characterized by the attempt of the international system to deal with the rise of Japan. . . . Let me briefly review the history. In the 50s the Japanese economy somewhat more than doubled. This is interesting, but not terribly exciting. It grew from small to medium. In the 60s it something more than tripled. This was unprecedented, and it grew from medium to large, and it began to have an impact. For example, in the United States we used to have a very large magnetic tape recording industry for home entertainment. One hundred per cent of that industry moved to the Far East. Not always to the Japanese, sometimes to Taiwan or South Korea. We had a very large radio industry, the largest one in the world, for home entertainment. Eighty per cent of that industry moved to the Far East. Now, one of the things that results from growing larger is that you make waves – statistically at least. The economy is now 200 billion dollars.[1] By 1975, in five years, it would be 350 billion,

[1] We refer to one billion as 1,000,000,000, and one trillion as 1,000,000,000,000. This usage will prevail in the following pages.

11

which is about the size of the European Economic Community today. That's a large economy and its effects will be widely felt. By 1980 it should be about the size of Russia today, about 600 billion.

Turning to issues of technology, Dr Kahn continued:

I would argue that most of the problems we face today, including pollution, can be met with a combination of more progress, engineering, proper design, money and some self-restraint. But unless you have an increasing gross national product, you cannot deal with these problems. In other words, you cannot stop. This accumulation of scientific and technological knowledge, this institutionalization of change, this increasing rapidity of change, increased universality, all these things are in the system and while they can be better controlled than they have been in the past they probably cannot be stopped.

The study is divided into six subsections: four on regional developments in Europe, North America, Latin America, and Asia; and two on central control areas: first, the rapidly changing world monetary, trading and foreign aid rules and practices and second, possibly the most critical single factor in the external environment of the 1970s, world capital shortage.

The second broad section covers four central responses that may be vital to corporate survival in coming years: breaking down nationalistic prejudices within the firm, as expounded by Howard Perlmutter; developing adequate corporate strategic planning processes, as explained by Igor Ansoff; employing computers for more useful marketing information systems, as outlined by Arnold Amstutz; and creating management development programmes, as explained by Bohdan Hawrylyshyn, so as to avoid shortages of capable executive talent as a restraint on future corporate growth.

Business International, as a processor of business information for multinational management, undertook the basic study for this work, which was written by its senior vice president, William Persen. The finished book was compiled by Thomas Aitken, incorporating material presented at the Davos Symposium, which was designed by the Centre d'Études Industrielles – the Geneva centre for education of international management.

PART ONE

ENVIRONMENTAL SURVEYS

CHAPTER 1

Europe

For the international corporation, no continent changed as much as Europe during the past two decades. And no continent will change as much in the next two decades. Western Europe, so recently the arena for repeated, highly destructive intracontinental wars, will form something between a semicomplete political union and a federation in which there will be a single market and considerable power left in the hands of national governments.

The latter is more likely, but it would include a single external tariff and no internal tariffs for any manufactured goods, something approaching monetary and currency unification, and harmonization of taxes and most other laws affecting business activity, including those affecting the actions of companies with parents domiciled outside Europe. In other words, the powers left to national governments will be highly circumscribed in any matters relating to economic affairs, though politicians and people will still be thinking, if not acting, in terms of the outmoded nation state.

But Europe is not becoming a Garden of Eden for the international corporation. Rather, the new opportunities stemming from increasing affluence, rising living standards, and economically integrating markets, are balanced by a lengthy list of growing challenges.

Rising competition on the rapidly unifying European market will be the key factor in shaping business decisions, government economic policies, and public reactions. International companies will see competition as a positive force for adopting Europewide strategies and structures. But many European governments, still reasoning essentially in terms of narrow domestic interests, will resist competition by ever-less-effective protectionist measures. Some of them may attempt broad reforms, e.g. 'participation', which may backfire and eventually imperil political stability. Strikes by workers fearing automation and plant rationalization, and unrest among students scorning the 'consumption society', but in effect deeply concerned about their own future, will further complicate the task of corporate planners.

If companies can expect the going to be bumpy, particularly in the next few years, there are nevertheless several reasons for optimism. European markets will continue to grow healthily – corporate planners can count on an average GNP growth for western Europe as a whole of 4 per cent a year during the period, with the greatest increases to be registered in 1972–74 and towards the end of the decade (see Table 1.I).

TABLE 1.I *Europe's Basic Statistics of the 1970s*

	Population		GNP		Per Capita GNP	
	1968	1980 (est.)	1968	1980 (est.)	1968	1980 (est.)
	(in millions)		(in 1968 $ billions)		(in 1968 $)	
Belgium-Lux.	10·0	10·5	21·7	35·8	2,170	3,410
France	50·0	54·8	126·6	227·4	2,532	4,150
Germany	60·2	64·0	132·2	237·4	2,196	3,709
Italy	52·8	57·8	74·8	142·2	1,417	2,460
Netherlands	12·7	14·8	25·2	45·3	1,984	3,060
EEC total*	227·9	259·3	396·7	720·0	1,741	2,777
Austria	7·3	7·7	11·4	19·3	1,562	2,506
Denmark	4·9	5·3	12·4	19·9	2,531	3,755
Norway	3·8	4·3	9·0	14·4	2,368	3,349
Sweden	7·9	8·5	25·6	43·4	3,241	5,106
Switzerland	6·1	6·7	17·2	26·0	2,820	3,881
UK	55·3	59·0	102·1	154·3	1,846	2,615
Finland	4·7	5·3	8·0	12·8	1,702	2,415
EFTA total†	92·8	107·0	191·1	300·0	2,059	2,804
Spain	32·4	35·8	25·2	47·9	778	1,338
Europe total‡	363·0	405·0	615·9	1,073·0	1,697	2,649

* Including Greece and Turkey.
† Including Portugal and Iceland.
‡ Including Ireland.

FACTORS AFFECTING THE EUROPEAN BUSINESS SCENE

General

Political Stability. While Western Europe has its potential trouble spots such as Italy, Belgium, and Ulster, political stability is likely for the region as a whole. Violent action between countries is highly unlikely.

Greater Geographical 'Specialization' of Industry. Growing competition will increasingly force large firms to invest wherever conditions are best. Whether governments like it or not, companies will thus bring about a Europewide division of labour, ignoring national borders, plans, or traditions. There are already several striking examples of such specialization: the concentration of petrochemical investments in the Antwerp–Rotterdam–Amsterdam area, the choice of Alsace by several pharmaceutical firms, and the growing attraction of Bavaria for electronics companies. Indeed, governments will try to influence companies, particularly foreign investors, to invest in poor areas (e.g. the Mezzogiorno or Brittany). But ultimately northern Europe will become the preferred site of capital-intensive industries, such as chemicals, metals, and machinery, while light industries such as foodstuffs, clothing, and electronics will increasingly move to the western and southern parts of Europe where labour is more abundant and cheaper.

Enlargement of Companies through Domestic Mergers. The drive to corporate concentrations in Europe will accelerate. But mergers will continue to take place primarily between national firms, at least during the next few years. By 1975, each major European country will have only one or two giant enterprises in the most technically advanced sectors. Although it is premature to speak of the formation of real conglomerates in Europe, diversification into other product fields (e.g. oil companies diversifying into allied fields such as chemicals) has already become and will continue to be the chief *raison d'être* of many national mergers, particularly in the United Kingdom. The present strong trend toward Europewide service companies (banking, insurance, transport, marketing) will continue.

More Cross-border Alliances. More and more European-based firms will seek partners across borders to form groups of international dimension. But genuine cross-border mergers (as opposed to acquisitions) between firms of similar size will remain rare for many years to come because of obstacles such as conflicting national company laws, unfavourable capital gains tax systems and, more importantly, because of obstruction by governments for reasons of prestige, unemployment, or national security. To circumvent these artificial barriers to Europewide concentration, firms resort to imaginative and often complex formulas that play down equity control to please governments and avoid tax problems, but give the partners the same advantages of mass production, purchasing, and marketing they would derive from actual mergers. These formulas normally represent a combination of several elements: joint holding companies owning the two parents' manufacturing subsidiaries (e.g. Agfa–Gevaert), limited cross-ownership agreements between the two parents (Dunlop–Pirelli), joint management committees, joint purchasing and manufacturing of parts, reciprocal distribution agreements or merger of the parents' international sales network, and adoption of common trademarks. The biggest obstacle to cross-border mergers – psychological phobias – will decrease substantially.

Broader R & D Pools. Companies in Europe will increasingly join forces in the area of research and development. To save costs, many firms will also set up joint technical information centres, particularly for aerospace and defence industries. An example is the Brussels-based International Data, a 'study company' formed jointly by the UK's International Computers Ltd., France's Cie Internationale pour l'Informatique, and Control Data Corp. of the US. Prospects are bright for companies to benefit indirectly from Europewide scientific associations (e.g. Europ-control) or non-corporate research projects. Ultimately the Six will join other European countries to form a 'European Technological Community' to pool resources in a variety of scientific and technological fields such as computers, advanced chemistry, biochemicals, oceanography, and rare metals.

Greater Attention to Market Dominance. Although European governments will continue actively to promote corporate mergers, antitrust authorities will watch the newly formed giants to make sure that they do not maintain artificially high prices. To prevent potential abuses, the EEC Commission may request that all mergers between large Common Market firms be submitted for prior approval to prevent oligopolistic groups from imposing excessive prices. Fines will be levied on price-fixers. While Europe will remain less restrictive in limiting mergers than the US, Germany is beginning to move in this direction, as is the EEC Commission in its attack on Continental Can.

Concern over US Investment. With the exception of unsophisticated countries, US investments will not be excluded on the childish ground that 'decisions taken in Detroit or San Francisco endanger national independence'. But European governments will look with concern at the increasingly adverse effect of US investment on their own balance of payments. Dividends paid by foreign subsidiaries to their US parents have been growing by an average of 10 per cent a year, and total remittances from European subsidiaries could amount to $5 billion or more a year by the late 1970s. Hence, countries that have balance-of-payments problems may be tempted to counteract the growing outflow of dollars by imposing direct limitations on new US investment and/or force local US-owned subsidiaries to export a large share of their output to hard-currency countries, including the US.

Marketing and Consumption

Enrichment of the Individual Consumer. Incomes generally will continue to rise rapidly, boosting consumer expenditures significantly. Corporations look for increasing sales of new cars, greater variety of models, more frequent model changes, and the upgrading of small-car owners to larger models. They expect rapid growth of large supermarkets handling larger assortments and expanding into non-food lines; growing acceptance and use of convenience foods; growing retailers' pressure on national-brand manufacturers and food processors to provide cut-rate prices and private labels; larger food advertising expenditures, emphasizing the growing need for good product design, more reliance on loss leaders, multipack deals, and special promotions. They can count on an average annual increase in per capita consumption of about 5 per cent; growing pressures from discount houses in the small appliances market and in the brown and white durables market; and rapid growth for colour television. Plans are for growing expenditures on clothing and footwear, furniture, household furnishings, watches, sporting goods, do it yourself supplies, and travelling accessories (and on tourism).

Increasing Medical Care Expenditures. Medical treatments to prolong human life are costing more and more money. The other factor boosting medical expenditures is more sociological in nature: the less-favoured classes will want to enjoy, as do richer people, the possibility of prolonging their lives. Equality in life will replace equality in death as a factor of social peace.

Concentration of Markets. Partly as a corollary of industry 'specialization' and partly as a result of continued urban emigration, the gap between the rich industrial areas of northern Europe and the poorer peripheral regions, e.g. southwestern France and Sicily, will widen. When drafting their sales targets for the next several years, companies note that affluence and therefore purchasing power will be increasingly concentrated in some segments of Europe, such as the industrial area represented by the Dunkirk–Basel–Amsterdam triangle and the circular area surrounding Copenhagen–Malmo–Goteborg.

Rising Sales Costs. As more European firms develop their sales in neighbouring countries, good salesmen, already scarce, will become harder to find and they will command higher salaries. To attract more sophisticated consumers, manufacturers will have to spend more money on advertising, particularly for TV time – now becoming increasingly available in Europe. Heavier taxation (mainly indirect), high borrowing costs, and longer credit terms for customers will hike manufacturers' sales costs further. To keep a rein on soaring costs, companies will have to hire only highly specialized salesmen and instruct them to concentrate their efforts on large-volume orders. And although the current shift from independent distributors to company sales networks will continue, firms that want to cover all of western Europe will have to rely on middlemen to serve important but peripheral markets, including some within the major population centres where competition is intense and/or distribution inefficient.

Improvement of Retail Distribution Channels. Supermarkets, chain stores, mail-order houses, and discount stores will mushroom, squeezing out the classic small shops and open-air markets and forcing manufacturers to abandon resale price maintenance. The biggest changes will take place in the suburbs of large cities, where giant shopping centres with ample parking facilities will be erected. The most aggressive retail and wholesale organizations will increasingly form Europewide purchasing cooperatives to buy more cheaply in bulk, and to broaden their assortment of goods. Again, this will mean sales opportunities for international companies but it also portends some dangers. These cross-border associations of merchants like to sell their products under their own Europewide brandnames.

Higher Disbursements for Defence. As the US reduces European military commitments, many European countries, Germany in particular, will have to increase their military expenditures. More money will be spent on acquiring new hardware or on conducting research for new weaponry. Sales and investment opportunities will open to firms that can produce for this growing market.

Increasing Opportunities in Eastern Europe. The economies of the socialist countries will continue to move in the direction of greater management decentralization, less rigid planning, increased emphasis on consumer goods, and more extensive trade relations with the West, while some forms of private enterprise will develop. Now is the time for western companies to prepare for events that will make the socialist countries, including even the USSR, possible fields for direct investment in capital, know-how, and managerial expertise at the end of the 1970s.

Labour and Unions

Increased Labour Costs. The rising cost of living and pressure for a larger cut of the income pie will continue to force corporations to pay higher wages, especially to skilled workers who will remain scarce. Employers in western Europe can count on an average annual 7 per cent rise in the wage bill over the next decade, as a minimum. While discrimination against equal pay for women continues in the Latin countries (France, Italy, and Spain), the gap will narrow.

Very Slow Progress in Labour Mobility. Labour mobility within western Europe will continue to be hampered by a flock of legal, linguistic, psychological, and economic obstacles despite efforts to promote it. But more people living close to borders will commute

21

TABLE 1.II   *East European*
(Average annual growth

	Bulgaria			Czechoslovakia			East Germany		
	1966-70		1971-75	1966-70		1971-75	1966-70		1971-75
	Plan	Actual	Plan	Plan	Actual	Plan	Plan	Actual	Plan
National income	8·5	8·2	8·5	4·1-4·4	6·8	5·0	5·5	5·2	4·7-5·1
Consumption	7·0	7·3	—	—	5·5	5·0-5·4	4·5	4·5	3·9-4·2
Fixed investment	11-12	10·0	6·0	5·6	8·3	6·0-6·5	8·0-8·7	9·7	5·0-5·4
Industrial production	11·2	11·1	9-10	5·6	6·5	6·0-6·4	—	6·5	6·0-6·4
A: Producer goods	—	11·8	—	—	6·7	—	—	7·2	—
B: Consumer goods	—	10·7	8·5	—	5·9	—	—	4·7	3·9-4·2
Electric power	—	13·6	9·0	7·4	7·1	6·8	—	—	5·4-5·9
Iron and steel	—	17·8	—	—	—	—	—	—	6·5-7·0
Engineering	20·1	15·7	17·0	7·4	9·0	7·5	—	—	7·0-7·5
Chemicals	24·6	21·1	—	8·7	9·5	10·0	—	8·5	8·0-8·5
Light industry	8·5	10·6	—	3·5	5·1	4·6	—	—	5·7
Food industry	7·0	5·8	—	3·2	3·5	3·4	—	—	3·4
Productivity in industry	5·8	6·8	—	4·7	5·5	5·4-5·7	6·5-7·0	5·7	6·1-6·5
Construction	—	12·7	—	—	7·5	6·7	—	7·9	5·0-5·3
Agriculture	5·4	3·1	3-3·7	2·8	4·8	2·7	2·5-2·8	1·0	—
Domestic trade	7·0	8·7	6·5-7	—	6·5	5·0-5·4	—	4·6	—
Foreign trade	10·5	10·3	12·0	5·7	7·1	7·2	7·3	9·6	—
Imports	—	9·2	9·8	—	7·1	—	—	10·9	—
Exports	—	11·3	14·2	—	7·0	—	—	8·5	—

— not available
Source: National plans and plan fulfilment reports.

every day to work in neighbouring countries (e.g. workers from Alsace crossing the Rhine to work in Germany and Switzerland). There will also be growing emigration from the countries of the Mediterranean basin. However, new trends are evident in the UK, where government agencies are proposing employment opportunities in Western Germany for certain skilled categories of worker.

Multinational Union Action. Manufacturing companies operating in several parts of Europe find themselves face to face with concerted cross-border labour demands and multicountry strike movements. Some US chemical and automobile corporations, Philips of the Netherlands, Saint-Gobain of France, and Hoechst of Germany, for example, have already discovered that the unions with which they signed agreements in one national territory have met with their counterparts in other countries (where the firms have subsidiaries and affiliates) in order to plan cross-border demands. These as yet loose liaisons are being established to prevent international corporations from switching production from country A to country B when faced with labour troubles in A. As the labour-in-management concept slowly makes progress in western Europe, unions will

Five-Year Plans
rates, per cent)

Hungary			Poland			Rumania			USSR		
1966-70		1971-75	1966-70		1971-75	1966-70		1971-75	1966-70		1971-75
Plan	Actual	Plan	Plan	Actual	Plan	Plan	Actual	Plan	Plan	Actual	Plan
3·5-3·9	6·8	5·5-5·8	6·0	6·0	6·7	7·0	7·7	11-12·7	6·6-7·1	7·6	6·5-7·0
3·4-3·7	5·3	5·5	4·9	5·0	6·7	—	—	—	6·7	7·0	7·0
5·4	10·4	5·5	6·8	8·5	6·7	10·3	10·5	—	7·4	7·3	6·5-7·0
5·7-6·3	6·2	6·0-6·5	—	—	8·2-8·4	10·7-11·6	11·8	11-12·3	8·0-8·4	8·5	7·2-7·9
—	5·7	—	8·2	9·5	8·6	11·2-12·1	12·7	—	8·3-8·7	8·6	7·1-7·9
—	6·6	10-11	6·4	6·6	7·3	9·8-10·5	9·9	—	7·4-7·9	8·2	7·3-8·2
—	7·6	—	8·2	8·6	8·3	16-16·3	17·1	9·5-10·5	—	9·1	6·8-7·7
—	—	—	5·2	5·3	—	12·7-13	12·1	9·5-10	—	—	4·5-5·5
7·3	7·7	—	10·1	12·9	10·9	14·6	15·9	17·0	9·7-11·2	11·8	11·7
9·4	11·7	—	12·5	13·2	—	18·5	21·4	22·0	14·8	12·2	11·7
4·1	4·6	—	—	—	9·6	8·9-9·9	11·6	—	7·0	8·5	6·2-7·0
5·4	4·3	—	3·9	2·7	—	8·9-9·3	6·3	—	7·0	5·9	5·5-5·9
4·2-4·8	3·5	—	5·1	4·8	—	7·6	7·6	7·3	5·9-6·2	5·5	—
—	10·2	7·0-7·5	—	7·9	7·2	—	10·3	—	—	7·4	—
2·5-2·8	3·5	2·8-3·1	2·4	1·7	3·5-3·9	4·7-5·7	1·8	6·3-8·3	—	—	3·7-4·1
—	8·6	7·0	—	6·1	—	—	8·2	—	—	8·2	—
7·7	9·6	8·0	5·6	9·3	9·5	9·2	12·0	11·0	7·0	8·5	6·6
—	10·3	8·0-8·5	—	8·8	9·9	—	12·6	—	—	7·3	—
—	8·9	7·0-7·5	—	9·7	9·2	—	10·9	—	—	9·7	—

seek codetermination rights with international companies on a cross-border basis.

Finance and Management

A Unified European Currency. What will amount to a single currency in most of Europe will not be achieved before the 1980s.

Progress Toward a Unified European Capital Market. Although companies cannot expect the formation of a genuine European capital market over the next few years, Europewide financial cooperation is developing rapidly. One striking example already is the creation of flexible European service companies in banking, leasing, insurance, and factoring. As national central banks lose power to regional institutions, several cities (London, Zurich, Brussels and Frankfurt are in the lead) will become the dominant regional capital centres.

Increasing Importance of Eurodollar Financing. The Eurodollar will continue to grow as a source of all types of corporate borrowings at costs competitive with or more favourable than domestic borrowing. Eurobonds will be easier to float as a stronger institutional and regulatory basis is built.

Greater Intergovernment Supervision. Companies must reckon with greater intergovernment coordination and cooperation concerning examination of corporate activities throughout Europe. For example, tax authorities in individual countries will increasingly coordinate their efforts to ascertain that a company's claims and deductions in one country correspond to its activities in another. Similarly, government authorities will consider the possibility of influencing corporate decision-making on a European scale. Particular attention will probably be given to how governments can influence investment decisions of major international companies.

MAIN CORPORATE CHALLENGES AND OPPORTUNITIES IN EUROPE

General

Sustained economic growth to an over $1 trillion economy by 1980.

New equilibrium based on economic strength of the two Germanies.

Further unification of the European market for industrial goods, offering greater opportunities for rationalized production but also far greater competition.

Continuation of an artificial economy for agriculture.

General overcrowding and, as a result, growing problems of transporting goods and people, air and water pollution.

Inflationary pressures.

Manufacturing and Concentration

Rapidly rising costs of production, closing gap with us costs.

Tougher challenge from Japanese industry.

Diminishing resentment against us capital.

Increasing use by European industry of synthetic rather than natural raw materials.

More national mergers between large firms and more cross-border corporate pools.

Stronger pressure throughout Europe for more government regulation of intercompany agreements and mergers.

Growing industrial activities of state-owned holding companies, and multinational cooperation between them.

Marketing

Rising costs of marketing, less sales per promotion dollar than in the US.

Growing affluence of individual consumers but continuing efforts by governments to curb inflationary pressures (e.g. restraints on personal loans).

Rapid modernization of retail distribution channels with explosive growth of suburban shopping centres.

Greater sales opportunities in individual east European countries despite rising international competition.

Finance

Additional pressures on corporate profitability.

Further unification of the European money markets with national short-term interest rates tied to the Eurodollar market.

High interest rates with rates for long-term capital never falling below 7 per cent.

Something close to creation of a European currency and a European central bank.

Stricter corporate disclosure rules, possible establishment of an EEC body pattern along the American SEC.

Europewide government action to fight erosion of tax revenue.

Labour

Slow unification of the European labour market.

Sharp increases in wage rates with increasing scarcity of skilled labour and slow growth of workforce, especially in the UK.

Rising absenteeism and guaranteed annual wages.

Tenser labour relations resulting from rivalries among communist factions, and multinational union action against international firms.

Growing mobility of European managers, who will put emphasis more on profits than on products.

More participation, more labour influence on corporate decisions.

The Role of Management in the Destiny of Europe

DR OTTO VON HABSBURG

Nationalism is economically indefensible. It has contributed power-fully to Europe's loss of position in the world. By leading to over-estimation of the importance of the accident of birth in one place or another, or of belonging to some linguistic or racial group, it has greatly reduced the available pool of leadership. During periods of high civilization no one has ever put questions about a man's origins, his nationality, or the shape of his skull. As examples I need only mention names such as Eugen of Savoy in the service of Austria or Watts in that of France. Even in the last century the Emperor Franz-Joseph summoned the great liberal thinker Schäffle from Tübingen to Vienna in order to entrust him with the direction of Austria's social policy. Soon afterwards, however, it became impossible even for outstanding men to work anywhere but their own countries, so that a continent-wide distribution of work, though badly needed, became out of the question. Thus a blockage of talent was constituted such as not even a rich continent like Europe can sustain unharmed. And what was true of men applied also to an increasing extent to geographical orientation and capital. These restrictions necessarily diminished profitability because they hindered optimal investment; they subjected the economy to un-economic criteria.

Politically, nationalism was positively suicidal for Europe. More-over, it very largely ruined the reputation of our continent through the meaningless fury for destruction of our two twentieth-century European civil wars. It also brought about that hasty decolonization, carried out under the worst possible conditions, the consequences of which mankind will suffer for a long time to come.

THE LAST TWENTY YEARS

Contrary to many fashionable slogans, it must also be said that what has been done in this respect over the last twenty years was in many cases just as irresponsible as the worst abuses of colonialism itself. Certainly, it was time for many countries to become independent. But to grant it so to speak overnight, and unprepared, without a large-scale economic plan to be carried out step by step, was simply unscrupulous. Let no one try to excuse it by saying that the colonized populations forced us to do things this way.

Nationalism reached its bloody zenith in the hellish doomsday of the bunkers below the Reichskanzlei in Berlin in April 1945. Since that time the idea of a supranational union has come increasingly to the fore, though it has had to struggle against the relics of old ways of thought. At this moment we stand at an important turning-point in the road. In the eighth decade of the twentieth century it is going to be decided whether Europe can continue to play an independent role, or must finally vanish from the world stage. We can no longer avoid this encounter with our historical destiny. It has been rightly stated that the fate of Europe will have been settled by the time the children now beginning school have come of age – and it is relevant to remember that in most of the free countries in Europe they now come of age at eighteen. The facts show that this statement is no mere rhetoric.

Whereas we are today in the twentieth century in all that concerns science and its social effects, and can indeed perhaps already begin to see into the twenty-first, our national constitutions remain spiritually based in the nineteenth. The political institutions and government structures of our countries, whether they be communist and totalitarian, authoritarian or democratic, stem from the era of the steam-engine. It is as clear as daylight that in such circumstances they are not fitted to cope with the problems of the atomic age. In politics we are still writing with a goose-quill at a time when industry is processing data on the computer.

This being so, the machinery of state lags behind development. The building no longer fits the foundation. It only continues to stand because, as history is always showing, forms generally outlive their content and slogans their ideas. . . .

BUREAUCRACY OF A UNITED EUROPE

Our greatest weakness in the work for a United Europe is the lack of open opposition. The idea is loudly supported by all and sundry, but their deeds are often contrary to their words. Experience tells us that it is easier to storm a barricade than wade through a swamp. This, however, is what we have to do in our struggle against a nineteenth-century bureaucracy whose obstinacy is a convincing proof of the law of inertia. Their conduct admittedly becomes understandable when one considers how many posts could be abolished if we proceeded in a rational manner towards a union of Europe. Let us take as an example the comparatively restricted field of diplomacy. We support superfluous embassies in countries where we could be just as well represented by a general European consul. The colossal number of sinecures that exist today, and the fanaticism with which their holders defend their privileges, give an idea of the effective strength of this army of resistance, whose resolute stand against progress has already cost us so much valuable time.

By contrast with the visibly decrepit condition of most European states, industry and commerce have had to adapt more quickly to the new realities, partly because they are closer to life and cannot go on for long dumping the consequences of their mistakes in the laps of others. This has brought about an inversion of the normal course of events. Normally speaking, it is the function of those in charge of policy to seize the initiative, but on this occasion industry and commerce are marching in the van. This explains why, when the EEC and EFTA are doing well, we are still limping along politically twenty years behind the times. There is, of course, a certain danger in this. One cannot just hand over the management of affairs in general to commerce and industry, if only because they could not possibly master all the various aspects of life. But politics can in a few minutes tear down what commerce and industry have built up through years of hard work.

Side by side with progress towards integration, the European economy is also showing signs of adapting its structures to the needs of the twentieth century. Certainly we are still a long way behind some others, especially the Americans. But at least many of our companies are showing that they have the men and the will to adapt the larger continental community to our true potential. Here again it has to be admitted that without the right governmental policies even the best managements will fall far short of their possibilities. A poll carried out a couple of years ago showed that bureaucratic incomprehension and interference was the third most important cause of the 'brain-drain' from Europe. . . .

Here, in everyday terms, is the task of the modern manager in a contemporary company. In a world becoming ever more complex, he is more than just the head of a production machine. He is not only there in order to manufacture better and better shoes or electronic devices. As part of the élite in the truest sense of the word, it is incumbent on him to see further than the narrow daily round, and to act accordingly.

The company manager or director, standing as he does in the forefront of material progress, must recognize that in human affairs all things depend on each other. His duties can therefore never be too closely circumscribed. He knows, too, that our company structures have made possible such mighty achievements in recent decades that, while preserving their essential principles, and precisely in order to protect the first and foremost of these, namely freedom, new attitudes must be evolved. . . .

In Europe, the manager must not stand aside from politics – indeed, he should give to it his best. Politics does not necessarily mean party politics, as is too often thought. Properly understood, it extends far beyond party strife; it is service to the general weal and to the community of mankind. However, it does imply readiness to accept office when higher interests require it. The Americans give us a good example in this respect, which unfortunately, in contrast to some of the less praiseworthy qualities of our friends across the Atlantic, finds little understanding or emulation among us. It is a misfortune for Europe that the barriers between business and politics are here almost completely impermeable. The fault is on both sides, so that, as a politician, I would not care to say which is the more responsible. It is silly to recriminate about the past; more fruitful to look for a remedy. . . .

For us Europeans, and especially for the élite, politics means above all the unification of the continent. If we do not succeed in this in the next few years, our role in history is ended. Working for Europe is, therefore, not just a pastime, not just the hobbyhorse of a few intellectuals, but a question of life and death. In particular, it is vital that those responsible for guiding industry and commerce should realize that this is the most important of all their tasks. They cannot and must not stand aside; they must give an example and recruit support. They must even go out into the highways and byways, not to preach a revolution, but to convince their fellow citizens that the question concerns their future. It is up to them

29

to keep on pointing out that the old idea of the nation state is finally dead and that only two courses remain open to us, one of which leads to a united European Europe, the other to a colonial territory of the superpowers who must ineluctably sooner or later turn it into a battlefield. At such a turning-point of history, no one can afford any longer just to attend exclusively to his own little production figures.

The Future Economic Environment of Europe

DR GERARD CURZON
Professor, Institut des Hautes Études Internationales, Geneva
Faculty Member, Centre d'Études Industrielles, Geneva

The European movement had been preaching from 1945 onwards that the only way out of its various dilemmas was to unite Europe, and bring Germany under joint European control. The French government's far more sophisticated answer was the Schumann Plan and the creation of the European Coal and Steel Community. It is necessary to recall the high reasons of state security which prompted France to propose the ECSC and its supranational constitution, otherwise one might be tempted, as many are, to interpret it as the first step in an inevitable process ultimately leading Europe to a confederation. The ECSC, therefore, was in 1950 the only possible way open to France of containing and possibly controlling German heavy industry which, under the American impulse, was already showing sign of miraculous recovery. Jean Monnet, whose motives were far more visionary, was given the green light by the French cabinet for reasons of state.

If one forgets reasons of state one cannot explain why national governments, acting in the short-sighted way natural to them, should embark on a long-term enterprise involving their ultimate disappearance. The fact is that from time to time it has been in the national interest of some large European countries (France, Germany, now, it seems, the United Kingdom) to allow the European federalists a chance to apply some of their ideas.

The Community has not yet established a full customs union among its six members. It is, at best, a tariff union, since there is not one single customs administration, but four. However, this may be considered a mere technicality so it is worth pointing out that the Community's internal tariff disarmament has not yet resulted in the creation of a single market as far as the free trade of consumer goods is concerned. The proof of this statement lies in the fact that consumer prices still differ very widely within the Community; in some cases by over 100 per cent, depending on the product and the country. Household appliances, in Germany, for instance, are about half the price of those in France, while Italian and Dutch prices for household goods are considerably lower than French, German and Belgian. As far as textiles are concerned, Germans and Italians pay about one-third less than the Belgians and the French for them.

THE ABANDONMENT OF MAJORITY VOTING

The one step which was to have lifted the Community from the level of an organization for inter-state cooperation to that of a nascent federal union, the replacement of unanimity for all major decisions after the end of the first six-year transitional period, has not been taken, and there is little prospect of its being so. In June 1965 France left the negotiating table in Brussels, on the pretext that the Common Agricultural Policy had not been drawn up according to timetable, and for six months practised the 'empty chair' policy. In January 1966 the EEC Council of Ministers met in Luxembourg, the French being present, at the end of which meeting a communiqué was issued which altered the whole basis upon which the Community was built. It was reported that:

> The French delegation considers that, when very important issues are at stake, discussion must be continued until unanimous agreement is reached; the six delegations note that there is a divergence of views on what should be done in the event of a failure to reach complete agreement. . . . They consider that this divergence does not prevent the Community's work being resumed in accordance with normal procedure.

Once more, France had demonstrated convincingly that what counted in European integration was not the written agreement, however impressive, but national interests as perceived by national governments over time. The celebrated Hague meeting in December 1969, which marked the end of a second series of French sulks and inaugurated a spirit of reconciliation, did not reverse the Luxembourg agreement, and the principle of a French veto on Community decisions remains intact.

THE ENLARGEMENT OF THE COMMUNITY

Article 237 of the Rome Treaty states that: 'Any European State may apply to become a member of the Community', and indeed many have done so, and some more than once. The enlargement of the Community has been an issue, on and off, for ten years now.

In February of 1969 the British ambassador to France happened to ask General de Gaulle how he foresaw the future of Europe. When General de Gaulle replied that he supposed it would evolve into a large free trade area with the Community at the centre, he was quite within the line of thought developed by his foreign minister. All that had happened was that the Community, France and the General himself were reacting to business needs and pressures, and were slowly coming around to the idea that political disagreements on how to organize European integration need not stand in the way of a more rational economic organization of the continent. The strength of these pressures for a more rational organization of the continent may be gauged by the fact that it must have cost de Gaulle a considerable effort to envisage in 1969 what he had so effectively quashed in 1958.

Mr Wilson, however, preferred to hold out for full Community membership, in spite of the difficulties this involved for both sides, and over-reacted magnificently to de Gaulle's 'speculations'. He informed selected Community governments of France's treacherous anti-Common Market behaviour, when they had not only been aware of it but had even discussed and agreed upon the idea well in advance of letting the United Kingdom know about it. The members of the EEC immediately interpreted Wilson's move as an attempt to split the Community and, understandably, the subject of enlarging the Common Market from a trader's point of view in order to accommodate business pressure in Europe was taken off the agenda.

These facts are recalled in some detail because they suggest the lines along which the Community was thinking before de Gaulle's retirement, and presumably represent a rock-bottom minimum solution to Britain's attempt to join the EEC.

However, there is one subject on which the Commission worked and which contains all the elements necessary to make it a vehicle for establishing a European confederation: the issue of European monetary union, discussed on the basis of a report prepared by the

C

Werner commission. . . . In other words, we are now going to avoid surpluses and deficits between Community members not only by altering exchange rates and pursuing individual economic policies in order to achieve internal balance, but by altering incomes, prices and employment like in the days of the gold standard. I have suggested that the acts of union by which several of our large and small European countries were created inadvertently caused the impoverishment and gradual desertion of regions not especially well-endowed by nature for life in an industrial society, and that the establishment of a European currency union is likely to do the same thing on a larger scale. However, the Werner Commission is not only aware that such a possibility exists, but even views it with considerable sangfroid. I quote: 'Equilibrium within the Community would be realized in the same way as within a national frontier, thanks to the mobility of factors of production.' But how could redistribution take place on a European scale without a European government, responsible to a directly elected European parliament? And is it realistic to assume that Englishmen, Frenchmen or Germans, will allow their level of economic activity to be determined by a government in which they cannot hope to have more than a small fraction of the votes? Voters feel helpless enough as it is to determine the course of events, without wishing to dilute what remains of their power still further by placing power in the hands of a government where their voices would be reduced to one tenth or less of their strength in the national milieu. It is doubtful whether power of this kind will ever be put in the hands of a European government by democratic means. Democracy, designed for a city state like Athens or Basle, limps along badly enough in large countries like France, Germany and the United Kingdom. It would suffocate completely in a European federation. Popular feeling in favour of a united Europe does not seem sufficiently strong to override these objections and therefore I feel able to predict that a European currency union is unlikely to come into being. Speaking personally, I also think it is unnecessary.

Thirty Points for Executive Action in Tomorrow's Europe

BUSINESS INTERNATIONAL CORPORATION

General

1. Show greater awareness of social and environmental problems by such actions as:
   Donating time and money toward city planning;
   Allocating greater outlays for worker retraining and education;
   Using handicapped and hard-core unemployed;
   Spending more money to combat pollution; and
   Utilizing national resources as much as possible.

2. Count on survival of national markets for many products despite gradual elimination of differences in consumer 'tastes' and buying habits.

3. Hold board meetings occasionally in various countries and appoint nationals of several countries to the board of the parent to demonstrate that you are an international company.

4. Enlighten European governments on the aims, practices, and effects of an international company.

5. Appoint a company spokesman for all of Europe to explain specifically unfavourable corporate developments (e.g. plant closures or collective dismissals resulting from tougher competition). This may save time, effort and bad (or inaccurate) press.

Manufacturing and Concentration

6. Cash in on low costs of R & D in Europe by setting up laboratories in the larger markets (e.g. Germany or France) or in locations favourable for other reasons (e.g. Belgium or Switzerland for taxes).

7. Count on keeping labour during seasonal production drops; you will have to pay them anyway.

8. Check with local and supranational (EEC) antitrust authorities before consummating a large acquisition deal.

9. Re-examine negative corporate policies toward joint ventures with state-owned industrial firms.

10. Study possibilities of entering into European manufacturing partnerships with Japanese firms.

11. Assume governments will pressure firms into setting up new plants in backward or declining areas.

12. Plan on rationalizing production for a single unified European market.

Marketing

13. Organize small specialized headquarters in Vienna, Munich, or Zurich to prepare for sales (and possibly investment) in eastern Europe.

14. Weigh carefully the pros and cons of international agencies handling your European advertising.

15. Increase brand advertising to resist the challenge of private retail labels in consumer goods.

16. Investigate feasibility of automated equipment to store, handle and sort goods at lower cost.

17. Consider creating a small special marketing unit at headquarters to serve bulk orders by international customers who demand package deals.

18. Envisage creating two separate sales forces – one for discount stores and mail-order houses, the other for small traditional shops.

Finance and Taxes

19. Develop improved Europewide cash management systems. Check what banking functions might be handled more efficiently in house, e.g. a captive finance company. Examine what steps can be taken for rapid transfer of short-term surpluses to subsidiaries in need of cash.

20. Re-examine headquarters site locations against more tax and

fringe benefit harmonization within Europe and future space needs and costs.

21. Be wary of long-term purchase or supply contracts that may expose profits to shifts in interest rates or changes in exchange rates.

22. Attempt to arrange long-term borrowings so that, should interest rates decline, you can then refinance at lower rates.

23. Obtain your share of European money by publishing annual reports in various languages and cash in on your reputation by appealing directly to your employees, customers, and suppliers.

24. Review national and EEC incentive programmes (e.g. European Coal and Steel Community conversion funds) for low-cost loans for new investment, as well as tax waivers.

25. Take a hard look at distribution patterns for warehousing in free ports to save on early payment duties and for warehousing in countries that offer low-cost inventory financing.

Labour

26. Assume keener competition for all executive talent, and pave the way for future recruiting by giving support to education, offering part-time jobs to students, and lending executives to business schools for seminars and lectures.

27. Prepare to deal with national unions cooperating across borders to increase wages and fringes.

28. Eliminate time clocks at plant doors and pay only monthly salaries to all workers.

29. Consider launching stock purchase plans in order to maintain labour loyalty.

30. Stress plant automation and provide vocational training to alleviate skilled labour shortage.

CHAPTER 2

North America

UNITED STATES

The US alone makes up something like 45 per cent of the market of the non-communist world, and about 33 per cent of the market of the whole world. While these percentages are falling slowly, for the foreseeable future, what happens in the US to a great extent shapes what happens everywhere else. The European and Japanese markets are closely interrelated with the US. While there is feedback, these important regions are still dependent on the US rather than the other way around. This is true, even though the US is the debtor, owing ever-increasing debts to non-US holders of the dollars that make up the recurring US balance-of-payments deficits.

While no one quite knew what they were doing on that weekend in March 1968 during which the two-tier gold price was established, the US–European economic relationship of the 1970s will be quite different because of that decision. Exactly what the relationship will be is not precisely visible, but it is clear that the interrelationships are already far closer than they ever were before. If US inflation used to spill over into Europe with some time lag, it will now spill over much faster. And the same is true for the reverse. The monetary squeeze in the US in 1969 led to a monetary squeeze in Europe with a lag of only a few weeks.

Europe's economic health has never been bound so closely as with the US. In the 1970s, it will become even more closely tied together (unless the unlikely happens and currency inconvertibility again becomes the rule rather than the exception). The cyclical periods when Europe is growing rapidly will become more and more similar in timing with those of the US.

Before forecasting the growth of the US market in the 1970s, it is wise to take a quick look at the past. During the 1950–68 period, the US market has expanded very rapidly. GNP in 1968 was more than three times as great as it was in 1950 (up 204 per cent). Even in constant prices, GNP practically doubled (up 99 per cent), which means a growth rate at about an annual average of 4 per cent in real terms, with prices rising an annual average about half as much.

But there have been dramatic changes going on in the three major demand components within the economy. Table 2.I points these out.

TABLE 2.I

	Personal consumption (as a percentage)	Fixed investment of gross national production	Government purchase
1950	67·1	16·6	13·3
1955	63·9	15·4	18·6
1960	64·6	14·2	19·8
1965	63·3	14·3	19·9
1966	62·2	14·2	20·9
1967	62·0	13·7	22·7
1968	62·0	13·7	23·1

Over the period there has been a startling shift from personal consumption and fixed investment to government consumption. The volume and percentage increases over the period of each of these categories have been as shown in Table 2.II (in current prices).

TABLE 2.II

	1950	1968	% increase
	($ billions)		
GNP as a whole	284·8	865·7	204
Personal consumption	191·0	536·6	181
of durable goods	30·5	83·3	173
nondurables	98·1	230·6	135
services	62·4	222·8	257
Fixed investment	47·3	119·0	152
in producers' equipment	18·7	59·5	218
residential housing	19·4	30·2	56
Government purchases	37·9	200·3	428

Economic growth has been thoroughly unbalanced. The meagre increase in expenditures on residential construction is startling, as is the huge increase in government purchases.

The questions are: Will these trends continue in the future? Will personal consumption expenditure continue to lag? Will most durable and nondurable goods producers continue to be what cannot be considered growth industries? Will one of the brighter spots, purchases of producers' equipment, continue to grow more rapidly than GNP as a whole, given the removal of the investment credit?

The 1970s began in a period in which the keynote was not restoring rapid economic growth (as was true at the beginning of the 1960s), but rather the effort to stabilize, to reduce demand and slow down inflation. This keynote will remain the dominant theme of official planners for some time to come, barring the outbreak of new military complications.

Real economic expansion will slow very sharply and remain well below potential (generally potential is considered to be an annual real growth of 4·5 per cent) for several years simply because it will take several years of demand restrictions to balance the unwise overheating of the economy permitted or encouraged by government during the 1965–68 period. While the Democratic Party apparently consciously attempted to arrange rapid expansion timed for election years, the Republicans will follow such a path with less emphasis. They will for some time be attempting to correct the unwise economic policy of past years so that potential rates of GNP expansion can be regained.

The US economy will be growing at below its potential through the first half of the decade. It will probably expand at something close to potential during the second half of the decade. The rate of inflation should slowly fall in the early years of the decade, levelling off during the middle years, then showing a stronger upward tendency toward the end of the decade.

The Nixon Administration parallels the Eisenhower Administration of the 1950s. It will attempt to exert budget restraint and tend to avoid efforts to counter some of the most pressing and costly domestic problems. It will be the need to face these problems in the later part of the decade that will restore rapid rates of real growth (and of price increases).

CANADA

Although the Canadian market is less than one tenth the size of the US market, no forecast of North America can avoid examining its potential. Closely tied to the larger US market, Canadian cyclical patterns are very similar to those experienced in the US – what happens in the US more or less also happens in Canada at about the same time.

But there are some major differences in volume of growth. While the US economy expanded 6·4 per cent a year in current prices and 3·9 per cent in real terms over the 1960–68 period, the Canadian economy expanded 7·9 per cent and 5·1 per cent respectively. In other words, the Canadian market has been growing 25–30 per cent a year faster on average than the US.

Probably the main reason for this faster growth in Canada is the higher percentage of GNP devoted to fixed investment. In 1968, this ratio was 18 per cent, compared to 13·7 per cent in the US. This 31 per cent difference is more or less constant through the years, and compares very closely with the 30·9 per cent higher annual average growth of Canadian GNP in real terms.

It is expected that Canada will continue to invest a 30 per cent or so higher proportion of GNP in the upcoming decade, and that its economy will grow in real terms at about 30 per cent more each year. It is also assumed that the growth of the Canadian market will not slow as sharply in poor years as it does in the US. This would mean that the Canadian economy will experience more or less the same 1973–74, and 1977–78 downturns that the US is forecast to experience and also that economic growth will be a good deal faster in the second half of the 1970s than in the first half.

THE CHALLENGE OF THE US MARKET

The US, as the obvious forerunner in the process of technological and social change, offers the supreme challenge to business managers in terms of anticipating and preparing for new conditions of corporate life. The US is the most revolutionary society the world has ever witnessed, and only those companies will survive that are prepared to accept change – and indeed welcome it – and that exhibit the necessary flexibility to meet it.

The US, to begin with, is leading the rush toward specialization. The division of labour, a prime aspect of specialization, follows not only from the accelerating pace of technological change, but even more leads to the increasing scale of productive units. An important, if only one of many, result of specialization is the

41

continual debasement of the workman and even of the manager over the short run, with jobs regularly scheduled for extinction as mechanical and electronic processes are substituted for human action. For example, the specialized diagnostician in medicine, or the legal researchers in law, are in the process of being displaced by computers with superior stores of knowledge and better ways to combine facts to solve problems.

Those who welcome the process of change do not view this development with alarm. Specialization – and the rapid growth of knowledge, processes, and products – creates a steady and insistent demand for new skills and new combinations of skills. The optimists, therefore, confidently project into the future a trend of constant upgrading of the minimum average educational and skilled levels of the labour force.

The same process of change clearly spells the death-knell, in the US, for those industries dependent on unskilled labour, such as shoe and textile manufacturers. These industries are challenged either to find new processes of production that eliminate much of the unskilled labour, or retrain their workers to go into new fields (or, of course, to set up subsidiaries in less developed countries that desperately need labour-intensive industries). This is true if only for the fact that economic and political pressures – and the social conscience of humanity – will simply not permit such industries to exist in this country behind high tariff walls when there are hundreds of millions of people overseas who need employment, and whose countries do not possess the form of economic organization, the concepts, or the wherewithal to train or employ the mass of their workers in modern, specialized jobs.

But perhaps a more important challenge is contained in the fact that – as part of the specialization process – modern man plays parts rather than acting as something like a whole person. He becomes a commuter, a breadwinner, a consumer, a political participant, a joiner – and everyone of these parts may be subdivided in time and place. This suggests that the family, which has lost a great many of its functions and purposes, will regain a great deal of importance in the future – which should not be overlooked by corporate forward planning.

Urbanization has been a prime fact of economic life in the US as well as in other industrial and less developed countries for many decades. Indeed, the US in the past fifty years has witnessed the largest mass migration in history – of the southern Negro and the Puerto Rican populations to the north. This explosive growth of urban centres, with its enormous consequences for business planning, is finally beginning to slow down as farms and poor rural sections become depleted of people, and as the geometric growth of suburban America continues. Nevertheless, the fact of enormous concentrations of people in urban centres – or megalopoleis – will continue for decades to pose a prime challenge to business planners. The economic, cultural, psychological, and social (not to mention political) requirements of these urban dwellers have not begun to be met on a requisite scale, and to meet them will require a vast amount of ingenuity, capital, and business acumen. Finding ways to build business activities – for profit – in response to these needs will provide a supreme challenge to managers for many years to come.

Another aspect of the increasing 'encroachment' of government in American society is the impact on the individual as he is increasingly called upon to play the role of political man. Put another way, in democratic societies, and particularly societies where government is becoming an ever larger factor in the scheme of things, alienation and apathy are increasingly irrational. But alienation and apathy are precisely what we are seeing today in the US. What is needed, and what can confidently be predicted, are new forms of political activity and representation. It is becoming increasingly clear that the present structure of American political life is simply no longer responsive to the problems and needs of the various 'publics' in the US.

Of immeasurable consequence to corporate planning, particularly regarding products and services that will provide the maximum future profit, is the peculiar demographic configuration that this country will see for many decades to come – with a huge bulge in the younger age groups, particularly teenagers, and another huge bulge of older citizens. Closely related to the studies that this peculiar market configuration demands will be the increasing emphasis corporations will have to give to the social sciences in general, which are lagging woefully behind the physical and biological sciences and which, if properly supported and harnessed by private enterprise, can do much to improve the human condition, not to mention corporate security and profitability.

Part of the increased focus and emphasis on the social sciences will be the study of the meaning of 'leisure' as the workweek and workday become progressively shorter. This trend has fascinating implications for corporate planning. Never in the history of mankind have human beings been challenged to seek identity and satisfaction in life in anything but a work-oriented situation. The present challenge is totally new in the human experience.

Sheer consumption of material products – and especially of consumer durables – in a society of increasing affluence and leisure will certainly not be as robust and rapid as consumption of various 'adult toys' including home entertainment (here again, note the influence of the family), books, workshops, and transportation. Already, one sees increasingly affluent production-line workers banding together for tours of Europe, as a choice in their expenditure of disposable income, instead of larger colour TV sets or a third car in the already overcrowded garage.

Corporations clearly can do something – for profit – to fight this dangerous trend towards polarization of American society. Many of them, such as ITT, have long since enhanced their profits by contracting with governmental agencies to train and to educate. One of the most ingenious efforts in this direction was undertaken several years ago by CPC International in undertaking to develop and market a taped course that brings a total illiterate up to the seventh grade level in reading in 120 hours – without the need for an instructor. CPC's chairman sold this new departure to his board by suggesting that the company's business is to take raw materials, process them, and turn them into marketable commodities, and if CPC could do this for corn it could also do it for human beings.

Equally challenging opportunities confront corporations in the area of environmental control and development. Many of them are now turning their attention toward problems of pollution, housing, mass transportation, urban blight, and other afflictions of American society. There is little doubt that a major allocation of corporate resources in pursuit of these goals is under way – and will eventually transform the very nature of private corporations. Here again, today's managers are challenged to explore the role their company can and should play as a 'service centre' in meeting the critical needs of American society. As noted above, this will entail a shift in the attitudes and skills of business executives and a receptivity to new concepts and new institutions – such as the creation of joint ventures with governments; of troikas of business, government, and universities (or foundations); and of consortia of complementary corporations.

Such a fundamental shift of corporate activity will run headlong into the problem of the time span within which profit is demanded by the investing public. Any substantial move by corporations to attack the social and economic ills of American society will probably require an extended postponement of payout, as lush as the eventual reward should be. The question of whether the investing public, and Wall Street, can be persuaded to give profitability a broader definition is one that today's corporate managers should be giving serious attention. Among other things, corporate managers today are challenged to lift financial public relations to a higher, more significant level.

The following sets of action for corporations that wish to be the leaders of tomorrow in the US market are being considered by European and Asian-based companies as well as those established in the US.

1. A programme of continuous training and upgrading of both workers and managers. Technological change and never-ending advances in specialization will render obsolete not only more and more production-line, supervisory, and lower-management jobs, but will also present a steady and growing demand for new skills and new management capabilities. A broad-scale programme of training at all levels of the company, coupled with regular in-house promotion to new and better jobs, is bound to cut costs in the long run, reduce labour disputes, ease the scarcity of managers, and accelerate corporate growth and profits.

2. Deletion of products whose production cannot be automated, or transfer of their production to lower-cost locations overseas. The only other solution open to companies with high-cost, labour-intensive products is to seek tariff or quota protection, but economic and political pressures, not to mention the conscience of the nation, will be such that closing the US market to products manufactured in Asia, Latin America, and Africa will simply not be feasible over the long pull.

3. Reaction to the growing size of the US population, especially in the younger and older age levels. According to some projections, there will be 242 million Americans in 1980, 92·3 million of whom will be 19 years old or less and 23·1 million who will be 65 or more. Among other things, these projections – and the rapid social

and cultural changes in American life – suggest strongly the need for corporations to give more support to the social sciences, which are lagging woefully behind the physical and biological sciences, and to employ cultural anthropologists and other social scientists to help in product planning, personnel management, and other areas of business.

4. Analysis of the deeper business implications of leisure time. For the first time in human history, an entire society faces the need, individual by individual, of finding identity and fulfilment outside the work-oriented situation during much of their waking hours. The growth areas of the future will include 'adult toys' and 'experiences', such as travel and home entertainment: 'experiences' will compete with 'things' and services will grow in importance.

5. Emphasis on the family as a social unit in planning personnel policies and products and services. As the social, political, and economic structure of American life increases in complexity, the family will grow in significance as the only place where man can give expression to his whole personality. As such, it will remain the principal decision point for consumer purchases, and will constitute a market of growing importance.

6. Planning for deceleration of urban growth. With the depletion of America's farm population, and the continued rush to suburbia and exurbia, the explosive growth of cities in the US will taper off. Among other things, this will affect the supply of new industrial workers and give even greater stimulus to automation and instrumentation. Business planning should also stress the fact that, although the growth of the cities is slowing down, America will remain an urban civilization, and that her cities, as vital centres of diversity, novelty, and intellectual ferment, will represent prime markets for new products and services and offer sizeable profit opportunities for companies that join in amelioration or solving the problems created by the massive urban migration of the past fifty years.

7. Planning to establish some form of guaranteed annual wage, on greater government response to and expenditures on the lengthening list of social problems in the US. This means that inflation will be with us for years to come, simply because there are so many needs that cost so much. Management must constantly strive for greater productivity and greater efficiency to survive in the inflationary milieu.

8.   Observing new, emerging political forms and concepts, and their probable implications. The present political system in the US seems less and less responsive to the needs and mood of the nation. In a very real sense, America is in the midst of a revolution. Whatever the shape of the new political system that will emerge, it is likely to have two major new characteristics: First, it will be urban-oriented and not just city-by-city but encompassing clusters of cities. Second, political expression and power will increasingly be centred in subgroupings such as students, blacks and organized labour, at the expense of the two existing major parties.

9.   Watching the developing thrust and goals of the labour unions. The days may be numbered when labour leaders will take a passive or defensive stance and merely fight for a piece of the pie after management bakes it. They are likely to demand a voice in what is made, for whom, for what purpose, and at what price. 'Participation' in short, could very well leap the Atlantic – and bring pressure to bear, in particular, on the need to allocate industrial resources to meet pressing social needs. Some labour leaders have already suggested that they will share their voice in management, when they get it, with academicians and the public at large.

10.   Increased allocation of corporate resources, at a profit, to the eradication of urban blight, housing shortages, pollution, transportation, stagnation, deficient education, racial bigotry and strife, and poverty – which is best described as lack of productivity. Clearly, US corporations have a direct stake in finding profitable ways to attack the social, ecological, racial, and economic ills that beset the American nation.

11.   Improvement of corporate ability to communicate and work with federal, state, and local government. The sheer size and complexity of the US and its private organizations, and the rapidity of unsynchronized change, place social order and cohesion in jeopardy. Expanding government activity in and control of economic, social, and cultural affairs seem likely – and to insure the maximum freedom of management and least damage to corporate growth and profitability, business should communicate more, and more effectively, and be prepared to work with government in new ways and through new institutions.

12.   Raising public relations to a much higher status and giving it a broader purpose. Redeployment of corporate resources should yield handsome earnings – but with a longer payout period. Corpora-

tions will have to do much more to educate Wall Street as regards the imperatives of tomorrow's corporate behaviour. They will also have a formidable task in educating the youth, labour unions, academicians, housewives, and government officials to the imperatives it faces and the reasons it takes the actions it does. Business has done an abominable job in the past of explaining itself. Failure to do much better – and to put managerial, technological and financial muscle to work in improving the human condition – will mean that the larger firms in the US will increasingly be treated as giant public institutions under more and more public control.

CHAPTER 3

Asia

It is difficult to generalize about the future of Asia, so spread and divided is the continent. It does appear that the 1970s will see a sharp down-swing in political confrontations and the use of force, although internal political stability is hardly assured in many of the continent's markets.

Some new balance of forces is taking shape in Asia. A settlement in Vietnam will probably come in the early 1970s, taking the form of an agreement on elections and for the full withdrawal of us troops over a period. This would enable a period of some kind of nominal coexistence between non-communist South Vietnamese political groups and the Viet Cong, and would allow a major international rehabilitation effort to begin.

After that, Vietnam would probably be vulnerable, with the odds on the communists getting the lot. The question is: Which of the several species of communist leadership would emerge? There is no reason to suppose that the economic liberalism and willingness to experiment in economic organization that has affected the east European communist countries would not also be displayed in Vietnam, including overtures to obtain western technology and credits. A peacetime Vietnam economy might not produce a Dubcek, but an Otto Sik is conceivable.

It does seem clear that after Vietnam the us will hesitate to intervene militarily in any Asian conflict, except in a clear case of external aggression covered by treaty commitments. At the same time, the us scaledown of forces will be gradual in some areas (e.g. Thailand) to give countries more time to strengthen their own defences. Thailand's guerrilla war in the northeast is serious, but it does appear to be controllable. Guerrilla warfare would probably continue, too, in divided Laos and could erupt in racially divided Malaysia; the area where us troops might remain in greatest force would be South Korea. All this will proceed at a time when China, the major potential external threat to most Asian countries, is looking west to its frontiers with the USSR. This confrontation is one of the major geopolitical facts of the 1970s and is not going to be resolved quickly nor easily; it could lead to conflict, more likely on Russian initiative than Chinese, but probably not this side of Mao's death. Even in the event of amicable solution in the near future, China is unlikely to deploy its forces against its other neighbours (as it did against India in 1962).

China needs to give long overdue attention to many pressing internal problems, notably economic growth, which suffered a massive retreat during the 'Great Leap Forward' launched in 1958, and then suffered again during the prolonged turmoil of the Cultural Revolution. China's external policies toward its neighbours in the 1970s will soften perceptibly, whatever the course of its dispute with the USSR. If the dispute remains hot, it would not want trouble on other frontiers nor with other powers; if the dispute cools and China turns to its economic tasks, it will need to pursue economic links with the capitalist West, as recent events have witnessed.

FIGHTING WITH RICE

The next feature of the Asian scene in the 1970s (and a very encouraging one for companies) will be widespread attempts to use enhanced economic growth as a substitute for military force. Guerrillas will be fought militarily when necessary in Thailand, Laos, and elsewhere, but against a background of economic development designed to alleviate the poverty and despair that provides the social basis of insurrection. The emphasis will shift from fighting communism with weapons to fighting it with rice. Probably the most visible demonstration of this will be in the reconstruction of postwar Vietnam, with massive international resources poured in to speed up development of the whole Mekong River basin area, affecting Laos, Cambodia, and Thailand, as well as Vietnam.

Here is where Japan will step boldly onto the Asian stage. The agreement between President Nixon and Prime Minister Sato for the return of Okinawa in 1972 envisages Japan remaining under much the same US defence umbrella as at present. Japan, at the same time, recognizes an obligation to play a bigger part in ensuring the security of the Asian region. But it will not do so by assuming a significantly bigger military role; it will make its contribution via greatly increased technical and capital assistance to the area.

This division of labour between Japan and the US in ensuring the security of the Asian region should bring wry smiles to the faces of US executives. With some shift of magnitude, emphasis, or deployment of its forces, the US will assume pretty much the same military responsibility for the defence of Japan (and probably Korea and Taiwan, too, since their defence – particularly Korea's – is fairly inseparable from Japan's). Japan will spur economic growth in the area. The US contribution is one of sheer cost; the Japanese one of business benefits to Japan.

Thus the stage is pretty much set for Japanese economic hegemony in east and southeast Asia, perhaps ultimately as far west as Burma. To the south, Australia will be more and more closely linked to the Japanese hub, though mainly as a supplier of minerals and other raw materials for the voracious Japanese industrial complex. Australia will also be the site of growing Japanese investment, but with an historical accumulation of some A$5 billion of UK, US, and European investment, the Japanese contribution in the 1970s will not have the impact that it will on the economies of the less developed countries of Asia, nor be so visible.

Japanese investment activity in the area will change in type as the decade rolls on. Today, much of it is typically directed at tapping raw material sources, mineral, agricultural, and fisheries (e.g. in Indonesia and Australia) but with some (notably in Taiwan and Korea) being motivated by the need to escape high labour costs at home by locating labour-intensive industries in lower cost countries.

As the years pass and as Japan's labour market becomes tighter and tighter, Japanese industry will shed its less capital-intensive, less sophisticated, and less growth-prone products into neighbouring countries. Put very bluntly, these countries will be making the outmoded product for which there is still a market (rather in the way that Facit decided recently to shift total production of manual adding machines to Mexico). This shedding of products and processes that are less than the most advanced will be part of a process whereby Japan will steadily upgrade both its industrial equipment and the quality and skills of its labour force.

All this will be accompanied by an expending network of Japanese financial institutions operating in the area. The yen enters the 1970s in a situation paralleling the Deutschemark of 1969. It is probably undervalued but, until Japan's import restrictions, its supports for exports, and its various exchange restrictions are removed, it is impossible to say for sure. The strength of the yen is that it will give Japan the financial muscle to take advantage of the investment opportunities that the new balance of forces in Asia gives it.

During the 1970s Japan will begin to exercise the political and economic leadership in the region to which her financial and industrial strength entitles her. Japan's GNP is already greater than the total GNP of the whole of non-communist Asia. Soon it will be greater than the rest of Asia's combined.

Japan will play the role of the main fulcrum of capital and technological inflow in all of Asia, in Soviet Siberia as well as China. Japan is the natural source of know-how and credits for such a development. Patterns for some of these ventures seem already to have been worked out, e.g. Japan providing capital equipment and know-how and receiving payment output of natural gas, timber, etc. What has been lacking has been Japan's ability to provide capital and credits on the scale needed, but this situation is now being remedied.

By 1980 this will have changed radically. East Asia will have become a Japanese sphere of influence in economic terms. Japan will be overwhelmingly the dominant trading partner of all of the countries in the region, just as it is already the major market for Australia, Taiwan, and Thailand. The rate of growth of the Japanese economy will determine the business cycle in nearly all the countries of the region. Japanese, rather than US or European capital, will be the major source of foreign investment in the region.

REGIONAL INTEGRATION

All Asian governments except India and Burma are committed to the idea of regional economic integration as a means of quickening economic development (and security, too). Some schemes are already being implemented (such as the Regional Co-operation for Development, linking Iran, Pakistan, and Turkey in projects serving two or three of the markets, or similar links between Taiwan and Korea in petrochemicals).

In southeast Asia, the next three or four years will show whether the idea of integration and regional cooperation has already taken root. Some start has been made through bodies such as the Asian Industrial Development Council, and more importantly, through the Association of Southeast Asian Nations (ASEAN), which links Malaysia, Singapore, Thailand, Indonesia, and the Philippines. The strategy is to cooperate on infrastructure, to develop industries jointly to serve the entire region and its 200 million population total market, and, as regional industries begin to produce, to eliminate tariffs product-by-product. The outlook for any of these regional market proposals reaching in the 1970s even the level of the Latin American Free Trade Association, much less EEC, is not particularly bright.

But the development of regionwide financial institutions and capital markets will play a significant role in Asia's development over the next few years. Most important is the Asian Development Bank which, in addition to granting loans for infrastructure and industry, is financing a study of Asian development issues in the 1970s and a major regional transport survey that will help set the stage for joint industrial development.

The Private Investment Corporation for Asia (PICA) was established in 1968 for financing industrial projects throughout the region, and several foreign banks have entered joint ventures in development finance and investment banking in individual countries.

Developing the Pacific

Japan's efforts in regional integration are largely directed toward the developed countries in the Pacific area, rather than to the less developed countries of Asia. Japan, on the private level, has sold the idea of a Pacific Basin Organization for Economic Cooperation and Development to the business leaders of Australia and New Zealand, who are now trying to enlist interest from Canadian and US private business organizations. So it is likely that by 1980 the concept of these five countries working together for development of the Asian and Pacific area will become a fact of life, very vigorously pushed by the Japanese government, and possibly by the Australian and New Zealand governments, too. But it does not presage any sort of free trade area among the five – merely joint action to bring capital and other resources to bear on the development problems of the area.

The most meaningful regional market will be the one resulting from the Australian–New Zealand Free Trade Agreement. This will proceed as scheduled, resulting in the major part of the trade between the two countries going on without the hindrance of tariff barriers. This, however, does not produce a very big market, although it is an affluent one in per capita income terms.

HUNGER

The spectre of massive famine continues to loom in many Asian markets, but it is doubtful that the race between burgeoning populations and expanding food production will be lost in the 1970s. Lord Snow's suggestion that there could be major famines in some regions as early as 1975 seems unlikely, although the population expansion will have all, or almost all, the challenging effects noted in the analysis of Latin America (see Chapter 4).

What is more worrisome is that the rising food production in the next few years may mask the longer-term threat and engender a false sense that the crisis has been overcome. One can imagine, for example, nations that have had some marked success in expanding agricultural output in the next few years letting up in the fight against starvation and once more turning the bulk of their investible resources towards more glamorous and prestigious ventures in manufacturing and other sectors.

THE GROWTH OF INDIVIDUAL MARKETS

Most of the market of non-communist Asia will continue to grow with some speed during the 1970s, although the pace of growth in a good many of them may be less rapid than during the past decade (see Table 3.1). Two factors that have been material in boosting growth rates in the past will be less powerful in the period under discussion. One of these factors is the flow of capital and know-how under official US and European aid programmes. The amount of aid as a proportion of GNP is falling and will probably continue to fall.

The other factor that greatly assisted economic expansion during the past few years is the vast amount of US expenditures in pursuit of the Vietnamese war. It seems safe to assume that these expenditures will be falling. There are no significant factors on the horizon balancing reduced aid and military expenditures.

TABLE 3.1   *Asia's Basic Statistics of the 1970s*

	Population 1968	Population 1980	GNP 1968	GNP 1980	Per Capita GNP 1968	Per Capita GNP 1980
	(in millions)		(in 1968 $ billions)		(in 1968 $)	
India	523·9	682·0	43·2*	74·8	82	110
Indonesia	112·8	152·0	11·5†	21·7	102	143
Iran	27·0	36·3	8·0	16·1	296	444
Japan	101·1	113·0	141·9	445·3	1,404	3,941
Korea (South)	30·5	43·3	5·7	14·4	187	333
Pakistan	109·5	147·0	13·8	24·8	126	169
Philippines	35·9	55·8	7·2	12·2	200	219
Taiwan	13·5	17·6	4·2	11·2	311	636
Thailand	33·7	47·5	5·0	9·5	148	200
Australia	12·0	14·6	26·7	52·1	2,225	3,568
New Zealand	2·7	3·7	4·8	8·6	1,778	2,324

* 1966.
† 1967.

Because of the overwhelming consequence to the region as a whole and to the world, three markets are specifically analysed.

Japan

The Liberal Democratic Party, which has ruled Japan for two decades, seems likely to remain in power for the foreseeable future. The only threat to its dominance is the Komeito Party, the political arm of the Sokka Gakkai religious sect, which seems to be taking over the chief opposition role from the socialist parties. Komeito's political goals are unclear, but it generally supports the 'little man', the consumer, and small businessman.

The chief problems facing the country include the growing labour shortage, particularly of skilled labour and managers; the increasing shortages of social amenities (e.g. highways, transportation, housing, hospitals, schools); and the threat of a widening technology gap as Western firms lessen their willingness to sell know-how except to Japanese firms they control.

But these problems do not appear to be critical in the face of the basic factors pushing toward continued very rapid economic expansion; a highly integrated nation, the loyalty of the average Japanese employee to the firm for which he works, the close partnership of government and business, the high educational standard, and the tradition of hard work and self-denial.

The labour shortage problem will probably be alleviated through continuing adoption by Japanese companies of western business techniques. Overmanning will be reduced. Automation will be greatly expanded. The present retirement age of 55 may be advanced.

The technological problem will be alleviated by a massive increase in government-subsidized research and development, although this development is probably ticketed for the later 1970s. There will also be profound changes in the university system – to counter the violence of the student demonstrations and to prepare students better for managerial careers.

There will be several important changes in Japan's external policies. Military expenditures will rise, probably to 1·5 per cent of GNP, and Japan will progressively take a somewhat more active role in the politics of Asia. Foreign aid programmes will be expanded to 1 per cent of GNP, with the greatest flow to southeast Asia. The restraints of the outflow of investment capital will be progressively reduced, as will the obstacles to imports of foreign goods and foreign capital. But reduction means less, not elimination.

In the past few years, forecasters have repeatedly indicated that the Japanese economy simply could not continue to grow at the hectic pace of the past (about 10 per cent a year for more than a decade). There seems to be no particular reason for predicting a slowdown. The 10 per cent figure appears likely to be a minimum for the decade as a whole. Slower growth rates in the US will mean that the rapid expansion of Japanese exports to the US will not be repeated during the decade. Asia, even with greatly expanded Japanese aid programmes, may not be able to continue its vast increases of Japanese exports of the past. But there is a very large potential for growth of Japanese sales in Europe, so large a potential that exports will continue to be one of the Japanese market's main push factors. Increasing investment in social capital will also keep GNP growth rates rising rapidly. The only real question facing the Japanese economy is its rate of inflation; if it increases too rapidly, it could force action militating against fast market growth.

The combination of rapid economic growth and almost static population growth means a steady and rapid rise in the standard of living. National income on a per capita basis in 1967 was $921, considerably higher than in the poorer countries of Europe and within easy striking distance of Italy's $1,020 or Austria's $1,093. By 1980 Japan's per capita income and consumption patterns should generally be on the same level as all but the most affluent of the European countries. The one significant area where there will be a gap in standards will be housing.

Tibor Mende, writer and commentator on geopolitics, has corroborated this evaluation of Japan as a major growing force in the last third of the twentieth century.

The first of five factors which Mende has listed as particularly significant is a planning system which is managed by an unofficial but meritocratic élite. This élite includes government, business, and banking interests and guides private initiative within the national policy that oversees the nation's economic life. This guidance is especially important in its influence on foreign trade and the role of foreign capital.

Second is Japan's extraordinarily high investment rate, compounded on one of the world's highest GNP growth rates. Taking the period between 1956 and 1963, Mende points out that the United States and the western European nations recorded GNP growth at annual rates between 3 and 7 per cent annually, while during the same years Japan's grew at a rate of 10·1 per cent.

Furthermore, while the percentage of GNP going into capital formation in the western nations ranged between 17 per cent for the United States and 25 per cent for West Germany, the yearly average in Japan was 34 per cent.

Third among Japan's socio-economic forces for progress is its potential pool of skilled labour. Some of this will continue to come from the land and will allow learners in the labour system to be replaced and move up to higher technological levels. Although about one-fifth of Japan's population is still in agriculture, the proportion is diminishing rapidly.

As it does, another change in industry itself is gathering speed. This is the modernization, amalgamation and absorption of the thousands of small enterprises which still employ two-thirds of Japan's labour force. As these industries become part of larger industrial complexes, their workers become available for skilled work. Although some economic areas already are sensing labour shortages, agriculture and the small businesses are still a resource that will support the economy for many years.

Another unique characteristic of the expanding Japanese economy is its banking and credit system, which permeates every level of economic life. Big banks lend up to 90 per cent of their deposits and big business goes to the bank for more than two-thirds of its financing. Government encouragement for the system takes the form of classifying bank interest as tax deductable but not extending the same treatment to security dividends.

Down the line the use of credit is prevalent, until the IOUs reach the small retailer. This paper is discounted by banks, giving institutions the power to shut off the tap or open it whenever the government may pass the word that restriction or expansion is advisable.

Fifth in the list of Mende's factors is the involvement of the individual with the group, be it family, business, association, and ultimately the nation. This loyalty towards collective achievement over individual interests encourages the long view over short-term goals such as immediate maximization of profits.

This positioning of a free enterprise capitalistic system within a paternalistic framework with a collectivist heritage creates strains, according to Mende, which will erupt as Japan's future problems.

One of these will come about as the Japanese advance towards higher technological levels tends to nullify the competitive advantage of its supply of cheap labour. At this point competition with other western nations will be more according to the latters' ground rules.

This same trend will impose upon Japan the need for greater investment in research, far greater than in past years when much of the nation's technology was imported. This will occur concurrently with an intensifying of the labour problem, augmented by a decrease in the availability of young workers as a result of Japan's years of successful birth control. Solutions rest in the area of automation and the great expense of its installation, or of massive importation of foreign labour which would be most difficult to absorb into the Japanese culture, or, as is already happening, the export of industries to surrounding areas where labour is more plentiful. Such regions are Korea, Formosa, Singapore, and other parts of Asia.

None of these solutions prevents a continuing rise in the cost of Japanese labour. Likewise, none of them will prevent the increased diversion of men and money toward a build-up of military resources which has already started. Although the first steps are modest, even tentative, there is a realization that Japan's access to overseas markets and raw materials should perhaps be protected by a naval establishment.

Another diversion, to be caused by more intensive competition on the technological level, may be a shift of commercial interest to the less developed markets. But, Mende points out, this can be accomplished only with injections of considerable financial aid with its inevitable strain on the nation's reserves. Meanwhile, the tremendous growth of the Japanese economy can bring about a shift to the western type of corporate self-financing, with a breakaway from present dependence on the banks.

A further strain on the Japanese system arising out of its very success is the growing consumer appetite. Even in the outlying villages there are television sets and washing machines where the simple life prevailed before. Increased consumer interest in the goods which Japanese industry is producing so efficiently erodes personal savings and the former, and current, great rate of reinvestment in the economy. And, of course, as personal ambitions grow the grasp of collective loyalties weakens, with the idea of individual freedom overcoming voluntary submission to the goals of the group.

However, it is Mende's view that when an Asiatic people executes a swing toward western ways it later reverses its course to embrace again the culture and folkways of its past and that there already are signs of this reaction in Japan. One is the much publicized suicide of Mishima, the great novelist who espoused the samurai tradition. It was followed by public adulation and the immediate purchase of all his works available to the public. While this in itself is not a proof of strong reaction, it indicates the existence of a tendency which may become more firmly outlined in the future. It will not, however, reverse a process which is making Japan one of the pillars of the world's future industrial establishment.

Australia

The market will probably grow even faster in the 1970s than in the past (5·5–6 per cent a year seems likely) sparked by the seemingly unlimited mineral resources uncovered during the past few years. Rising exports of minerals may well mean permanent trade and payments surpluses, ending the stop–go development of the past.

Australia will still face unstable weather conditions on its agricultural sector. More important will be the excruciating labour shortage. And the threat of powerful inflationary explosions will be a ubiquitous danger. These factors will mean a continued cycle of faster and slower periods of growth, but the slower periods are unlikely to be as depressing as in the past.

The Australian dollar will remain fundamentally sound. Even in the event of another sterling devaluation, the Australian dollar would probably not follow the pound. Australia holds less and less of its reserves in sterling, and what it does hold is guaranteed by the UK. Even more important, the UK as a market diminishes in importance as Japanese markets for Australian exports widen.

Australia will be linked more and more with Japan. The trade between them is rising very rapidly (mostly minerals to Japan) and will continue to grow more closely tied to Asia. Defence policy will still be a dilemma. Australia will keep troops in Malaysia–Singapore, but may be hesitant to use them if the need should arise; and it will press for continued US involvement in Asia while trying to retain some independence (by not signing the nuclear proliferation treaty, for example) in case the US should pull out.

China

Because China will most probably become one of the 'new' markets of the 1970s and because it is no doubt the world's least known, extended treatment is given here.

China has published no statistics since 1959. The work of charting the progress of its economy is a specialized, painstaking task for economic scholars. Virtually the only data open to inspection concern China's foreign trade. Details of the volume, composition, and direction of this trade can obviously be obtained from the published data of the countries trading with China. On any matters other than trade, there must be a high degree of conjecture about the Chinese economy.

Population is at least 750 million, with per capita GNP of something below $100. This is only a shade above Indonesia's and slightly behind Pakistan's. One estimate suggests that by 1980 China's per capita income will be only $120, partly due to economic growth on only a modest scale, but also as a result of continuing population increase. Gross national product is probably no more than $70–80 billion at present. (As a rough approximation, think of mainland China in total GNP terms as being somewhat smaller than Italy.)

The most important thing for the international executive to know about mainland China is that its economic and trade policies have very largely been the playthings of ideology and politics. Its erratic course of internal growth has suffered to some extent from bad harvests (notably in the 1959–61 period), but has been even more affected by politico-ideological decisions of its highly centralized and authoritarian government.

After the foundation of the People's Republic of China in October 1949, economic stabilization was achieved extremely rapidly. By 1952 GNP was back to its prewar peak. The first Five Year Plan was launched in 1953 and by 1957 industrial production was double the 1953 level and total national domestic product rose 33 per cent. The emphasis was on heavy industry, the growth of which far outpaced production of consumer items. Agriculture was neglected and in per capita terms agricultural output actually declined because of rapidly rising population (there was an increase of 70 million mouths to feed in 1952–57).

In this period, credits and technology from the USSR played a big part in making fast growth possible. China received the latest Soviet equipment, including entire plants and tens of thousands of Soviet technicians and skilled workers were in the country.

The Great Leap policies instituted in 1958 turned out to be one of the world's most spectacular economic disasters, comparable in effect to the 1929–32 depression. Things were made even worse by poor harvests for three years running.

One of the factors impelling the Chinese into the Great Leap was the growing split with the Soviet Union that was eventually to lead to the sudden withdrawal of all Soviet technicians and help from the country. The Great Leap was an attempt to industrialize (with emphasis on heavy industry) at furious breakneck speed with little consideration for available resources and a virtual rejection of the need for technology, priority planning, or other rational considerations. One estimate suggests that GNP declined 15 per cent as a result of the Great Leap; another suggests there was a temporary decline in GNP of as much as 30 per cent.

Recovery began early in 1962 with a switch of emphasis to agriculture, but it was a slow recovery. By 1965, national income was probably 7 per cent above the 1958 level and industrial production was above the 1958 level, but probably not by very much. This was achieved more by gradual re-employment of capacity installed before and during the Great Leap than by new investment. Within the industrial sector, emphasis was placed on the petroleum and chemical fertilizer industries; output of these in 1965 was probably five times greater than in 1958. But in per capita terms food production was probably lower in 1965 than in 1958.

Then came another setback to economic growth, again deriving from political considerations, in the form of the Cultural Revolution launched in 1966. This was not such a serious setback as the Great Leap, but it undoubtedly caused chaos in many sections of industry, transportation, and other services. One estimate suggests that national income in 1968 was no higher than in 1965, i.e. that the Cultural Revolution cancelled out any economic growth, but did not actually turn growth negative.

Calmer times have come to China now that the Cultural Revolution has begun to run its course. Judging from the considerable expansion of China's external trade in recent years, internal growth is proceeding once again.

Estimates of China's future economic growth vary widely depending on the assumptions made about its population control policies, internal politics, degree of tension with the USSR, and relations with the outside world. Pessimists suggest that in the long term it can only average 2 per cent annual increase in real GNP, while at the other end of the range there are estimates of around 5 per cent. Nobody has suggested that it could move into high gear and grow at the rate of Korea, Taiwan, or Japan with rates of around 10 per cent annually. Even on the 5 per cent growth assumption, it will remain a poor market in per capita terms for the rest of this century.

The one thing that might change this picture would be a shift in internal Chinese and international alignments so radical that the world community, communist and non-communist, will be prepared to pour in massive resources of foreign aid for Chinese economic development and that the Chinese will be prepared to accept such aid and apply it in rational priorities under guidance of the UN Development Programme and/or the World Bank. In a better world this could be one of the really great challenges for mankind in this century.

China as an Importer. Chinese spokesmen can be quoted as saying that foreign trade is inseparable from politics. There is evidence in support of both interpretations of China's foreign trade policy but, considering it all, the chief executive officer should act on the assumption that China's overseas trade policies will be closely aligned with politics, at least in the next few years.

In the 1950s, around 85 per cent of China's total foreign trade (i.e. imports and exports) was with the USSR and its allies; today, only about 8 per cent is with other communist nations. Both situations reflect political attitudes, not rational economics.

It is anybody's guess whether China will avail itself of the opportunity created by the US to buy products from US subsidiaries. If it does so, very likely some of the purchases will be made as political gestures in the context of Chinese relations with both the USSR and the US.

Foreign trade represents only about 3–5 per cent of Chinese GNP. But imports are decisive for industrialization, and at other times have been decisive for domestic stability, as in the 1960s when large imports of wheat and other grains were made to offset bad harvests.

China, perhaps more than any other communist nation, balances its exports and imports. Its foreign trade expanded rapidly in the 1950s when economic growth was fast, doubling between 1952 and 1959. It then declined rapidly during the Great Leap, recovered in 1962 and by 1966 was above the 1959 peak level. It declined slightly in 1966–68 as a consequence of the Cultural Revolution, and then underwent very rapid expansion. At its best, China seems to be a $2 billion importer, meaning that it is a much smaller foreign trader than most countries in western Europe.

Any expansion of China's imports (in the absence of credits) is dependent on expansion of its own sales abroad. These consist mainly of exports drawn from agriculture, possibly some minerals, and consumer goods industries. Chinese shoes, toys, canned foods, radios, sewing machines, and other consumer products are turning up in overseas markets, but the design, quality, and marketing methods are all extremely poor. Alexander Eckstein, probably the world's foremost expert on the Chinese economy, suggests that China's foreign trade might grow 40 per cent in the next ten years, meaning an annual addition of $80–100 million to imports.

OECD countries in recent years have provided up to 90 per cent of China's total imports, the exact percentage depending on the amount of wheat and wool purchased from Australia, and rubber from Singapore and Ceylon.

Generalizations about China's import patterns are difficult to make. Trends apparent in recent years may completely change in the future, depending on the whims and priorities set by Peking. If harvests are bad, China buys wheat and other foodstuffs (although sometimes wheat has been imported and rice exported in order to make a gain in foreign exchange at the expense of the people's dietary choices). Otherwise, scarce foreign exchange is used to buy industrial raw materials (rubber, steel, cotton, basic chemicals) or plant and equipment.

In 1966–68, chemicals, manufactured goods, and machinery and transport equipment accounted for 75–82 per cent of China's total imports from OECD sources, but over the years there were big swings among the three groups. Machinery and transportation equipment imports were $235 million in 1966, but slumped to $104 million in 1968. Over the same period, imports of chemicals rose 26 per cent from $205 million, and those of manufactured goods by 39 per cent from $277 million to $385 million. Mainland China's foreign trade expanded considerably in 1969 and is now set for further growth.

LESSER DEVELOPED COUNTRIES

Africa, Asia, and Latin America, the over-populated and underfed southern half of the globe, offers its northern neighbours their greatest opportunity and their most menacing challenge. Tibor Mende's economic analysis takes us further back in history and further along into the future.

Historically, Mende states, the supply of northern aid to the southern hemisphere has declined steadily from the days of colonial investment or even the post-war years of the Marshall Plan. Simultaneously, the burden of public and foreign debt carried by these countries has increased to the breaking point. Nor has their trade, although greater in volume, grown in relation to the world's total; it has not alleviated the misery of the less developed countries.

The most apparent solutions are: that some of these nations will benefit from the overspill of prosperity from richer neighbours; that they will seek or accept a client–state relationship with the wealthier northern states; or they will detach themselves from the global pattern. Finally, there are two possible scenarios for the future, an optimum and a minimum, with the probability taking shape somewhere between the two.

The emancipation of the post-colonial world, now called the lesser developed countries (LDCs), has been, according to Mende, a problem overlooked by anthropologists, agronomists, and sociologists, while being picked up by economists because they thought it could be quantified. Their thought was based on two assumptions:

one, that development is based on savings, or investment; two, that when a modern economic sector is created its influence will fan out over the surrounding area. These thoughts suggested that direct aid to fill the savings gap and increased trade to make foreign currency available would bring about the needed development. After twenty-five years, unsatisfactory results bring these theories into question.

Mende concedes that the three tools available to LDCs for their development are the mobilization of their own human and material resources, aid from outside sources, and earnings from foreign trade. Setting aside the question of local resources, Mende points out that the LDCs acquire financing in the proportion of one-fifth direct aid to four-fifths earned through trade and if the aid is diminished then the trade needs to be increased.

Moreover, since 1961, direct aid, increasing in amount by 2 per cent a year, has not kept up with population increases or the diminishing value of money. While the donor countries have doubled their own gross national product their contributions have decreased as share of gross national product to one-third of 1 per cent.

The public debt of the LDCs has meanwhile increased catastrophically. From a total of $10 billion for 97 such countries in 1955 the debt has risen to about $55 billion today and the cost of servicing the debt has jumped from $800 million to an estimated $5 billion a year. To this burden these countries have added dividend payments on foreign investments, charges for shipping and insurance, the costs of export credit financing, and other hidden expenditures which make them, in fact, net capital exporters, despite the aid they receive.

Mende states that the decline in aid is not overcome by an increase in trade benefits. Although the total trade in volume of the LDCs has grown, their share of the world's trade has diminished, as the significant gains have been made in interchange between the affluent nations. Figures are not totally reliable but the outline is fairly clear.

The current situation, then, is one of declining aid, increasing public debt, and a waning share of the world's trade. Such positive moves as the formation of regional markets have promise but not spectacular performance, partly because the countries who have so recently won their sovereignty are reluctant to yield any of it in such joint enterprise.

Meanwhile, new problems are arising and in a changing scene. One of these is the uncontrolled mass exodus from the countryside to already overloaded urban centres and the consequent emergence of explosive pressures in these cities. Even before the Pakistan situation, Calcutta was a prime example of this trend and that dismal city now seems destined to cope with the needs of 30 million people within twenty-five years. The populations of the Latin American cities are predicted to increase by 300 per cent in the next fifteen years, with results already forecast by the urban terrorism pre-empting so many of today's headlines. (See Chapter 4: Population and Urbanization.)

The doubling of population in the southern hemisphere by the end of the century will bring a second problem into focus: simply, how to feed this deprived sector of humanity. Feeding needy countries already consumes some of the energy of the affluent. Of immediate importance is the need to establish the conditions in which the 'green revolution' can flourish in the LDCs. Should the 'green revolution' not come off, however, one of history's paradoxes may occur. The affluent nations, diverting supplies of food to the LDCs, could well look for repayment in the form of industrial products. To make this possible, they would have to provide aid for the building of industries in the LDCs and thus inadvertently bring about an unsought solution to their problems.

Another problem already taking shape is the concept of private enterprise and its motivations in the spread of multinational corporate action. That concept and those motivations, running counter to the heritage and aspirations of the LDCs, may require adaptation to new forms. Multinational companies are already facing this situation and others will have to put it on their long-range agendas.

Tibor Mende concludes this discussion by presenting the outlines of two possible scenarios, one an optimum situation, the other, a minimum. The optimum situation would stem from a realization that the stronger states, having put aside the possibility of atomic conflict, should join in coordinated policies and programmes directed toward the LDCs. They would change their relationship with China, making it unfeasible for that nation to continue rallying the weaker states against their stronger northern neighbours. This would stop the trend toward isolation which otherwise might divide the world into competitive blocs: the Chinese with their

Asian satellites confronting the United States and its Latin American stable, Europe and its African clients, and Russia with the Middle East.

Ideally, the new coordinated policies would be carried out by international institutions who would avoid the humiliating processes of intervention. They would help restructure the LDCs industrially, encourage their development of regional trade associations, and bring them to the status of equal partners in the pattern of international bargaining. While the results might not be Utopian, they would diffuse the situation of the passion and despondency which now beset it.

The minimum scenario would contrast sharply with the developments just described. Putting short-term interests ahead of the long-range, the affluent nations would create pressures on China to lead an anti-white crusade which would change the prevailing forces in the world. The wars in the southern hemisphere, wherein the belligerent states act as pawns of the north, could intensify to the point where northern interests could become directly involved and the atomic threat would be revived.

Trade and aid policies as currently practised could continue to impose unsuitable technologies on areas beset with dual economies and the senseless urbanization in those countries would lead to further destruction, with Balkanization replacing even the incipient desires for regional cooperation.

Moving from hypothesis to prediction, Mende asserts that probably neither extreme will emerge but that something like the present situation will continue, with its proportion of successes and failures, its mix of countries emerging from the darkness while others dig deeper into their depression, and with the shifting policies of the north coming short of war without attaining peace, avoiding chaos without finding order, an interregnum holding within it the potential of some day moving toward the always promising optimum or the menacing minimum which stand in the wings of the world's stage today.

CHAPTER 4

Latin America

Latin America is a continent swept by social, economic and political forces of revolutionary potential. Driven by the inexorable pressures of a population explosion unlike anything experienced in previous history or in other parts of the world, and held back by the many handicaps of underdeveloped economies and the friction of conflicting political ideologies, the Latin American countries are straining their limited capital resources and human skills to achieve an accelerated economic growth commensurate with the rising demands of their impatient people. The resulting ferment of change and development offers challenging opportunities for profitable business contribution in the area, but companies must be prepared to accept the risks and cope with the problems of operating in an unstable environment.

The principal factors that will shape the future Latin American business environment fall under six major headings: the population and urbanization explosion; the financial bottlenecks that threaten economic growth; rising social unrest and political instability; economic nationalism, directed particularly at foreign investment; and continuing efforts toward regional integration.

The importance of the population and urban growth cannot be overstressed. It is not just one among several major trends, but the fundamental one. The growing repercussions of population growth – through the economic, social and political spheres – will make it an increasingly determinant factor in the other trends that shape the Latin American business climate.

POPULATION AND URBANIZATION

With population growth averaging 2·8 per cent annually (*about 1·4 times faster than in Asia*, and nearly three times the US/European average), Latin America's population is expected to climb by some 90 million during the coming decade to a total of 365 million people in 1980. This increase will be concentrated in the northern countries, with the population of Mexico plus Central America and the Caribbean expanding by about 38 per cent to an estimated 119 million, and that of the tropical countries of South America by about 34 per cent to 198 million (124 million in Brazil alone). The growth will be much slower in the temperature countries of the southern zone, especially in Argentina and Uruguay, averaging only 20 per cent over the decade to about 48 million by the end of the century the population of Latin America is expected to pass 600 million.

The problem lies not in overpopulation – the regional average of 12 people per square mile is still well below Europe's 19 and far below Asia's 68 – but rather in the tremendous social and economic strains inherent in the rapid rate of increase. The unprecedented growth experienced during the past two decades has had profound effects on the age-group distribution as well as the geographic distribution of the population, and has created a tremendous strain on the region's capital resources, which are clearly inadequate to cover its constantly growing needs for housing, education, health and social services, together with the productive investments needed to provide more jobs and raise income levels. All of this leads to overwhelming pressures for far-reaching government intervention in the economy.

The age structure of the population is shifting steadily, with an increasing proportion of children and adolescents. On average, 42 per cent of the population is now under age 15. This means a far greater demand, relative to the total population and economic resources, for education and other services needed by the young. At the same time, the economically active population is shrinking in relative terms so that there are proportionately fewer people to carry the burden of supporting the young and the other members of society who are not economically productive. In other words, the ratio between producers and consumers is increasingly unfavourable, thereby reducing the surplus of production that can be set aside for investment.

The geographic distribution of the population has been shifting even more dramatically owing to a massive exodus of surplus rural population to the cities. Between 1950 and 1960 the proportion of

69

total population residing in cities above 20,000 inhabitants jumped from 25 per cent to 33 per cent for the region as a whole, reaching 55 per cent or more in Uruguay, Argentina, and Chile. The proportion is expected to reach 60 per cent by 1980, with the number of cities above 1 million inhabitants rising from nine in 1960 to 27 in 1980.

Faced with the soaring growth of urban population, hard-pressed municipal authorities have been unable to provide enough employment opportunities, housing, water, sewage and electricity lines, schools and hospitals, or urban transport facilities. The results of this failure are visible throughout Latin America in the burgeoning slums where economically marginal urban populations live in makeshift dwellings, a breeding ground for social unrest and political upheaval.

The problems of feeding Latin America's growing population are less severe than in some other developing countries. Overall farm output has climbed by about 4 per cent annually since 1960 – more than fast enough to keep pace with population growth, though not enough to improve generally deficient nutritional levels. Nevertheless, imports of foodstuffs and other farm products have been increasing by close to 4 per cent per year. The ultimate problem of feeding Latin America's masses lies not so much in producing the food as in providing urban consumers with means of purchasing it. This leads directly into what is probably the most serious problem of all: that of creating jobs for the growing labour force.

Reliable statistical information on unemployment and underemployment is hard to come by in Latin America, but the most authoritative estimates put it at 26 per cent of the economically active population in 1960, and 30 per cent today. Moreover, the full impact of the post-war population is only now beginning to be felt in the labour market; the annual expansion of the labour force will accelerate from 2·8 per cent in the 1960s to 3·0 per cent in the 1970s.

Just to hold unemployment and underemployment at their present dangerously high levels, Latin America will have to create about 2·5 million new jobs per year in the coming decade, compared to an actual rate of 1·6 million annually in the 1960s. This would require an acceleration of annual economic growth from about 4·5 per cent in the 1960s to 6 per cent in the next decade – or to 7 per cent if unemployment and underemployment are to be reduced

to tolerable levels by 1980. Where such rates cannot be achieved –
and they certainly will not be achieved everywhere – the outlook
is for further deterioration in unemployment levels, with a consequent intensification of social and political tensions.

Since government cannot afford to view such a prospect with
complacency, job creation is bound to get higher priority in the
years to come. This implies a series of governmental responses
including encouragement of construction activity (a must in any
case); pressure on traditional, labour-intensive consumer goods
industries to expand their production (e.g. by reducing prices to
stimulate demand); modernization of rural economies to relieve
migratory pressure, with special incentives for investment in backward areas (e.g. northeast Brazil); restructuring of investment
incentives to foster more labour-intensive operations; and increased
attention to vocational training programmes.

In absolute (if not in per capita) terms, most Latin American
countries have achieved a creditable rate of economic growth
during the 1960s. The annual increase in gross domestic product
(GDP) in 1961–68 averaged 4·6 per cent for the region as a whole,
and more than 6 per cent in Mexico and several Central American
countries. Most countries in the region appear to have the potential
for significantly faster growth.

BASIC STATISTICS OF THE 1970s

The rapidity of population growth will vitiate relatively rapid rates
of overall GNP expansion during the 1970s in Latin America. While
total GNP for the region will climb something like 85 per cent in
real terms, per capita GNP will rise only around 30 per cent. The
market as a whole and each of its national components will continue
to be in or close to the less developed class in 1980.

Mexico, Brazil and the Central American Common Market will
grow most rapidly in overall terms, but Argentina will grow most
rapidly in standard of living terms, simply because its population
will be one of the more slowly expanding ones in the region.

The forecasts are sobering to corporate planners who might
otherwise get overly enthusiastic about the accomplishments of the
CACM and the Andean bloc. While both markets offer great opportunity and both will be growing rather rapidly during the 1970s,

neither are the big markets of the region, either on gross or per capita terms.

Although the problems of accelerating economic growth vary from country to country, the most serious bottlenecks for most of the region are financial – the shortage of capital and of foreign exchange.

TABLE 4.1

	Population 1968 1980 (in millions)		GNP 1968 1980 (in 1968 $ billions)		Per Capita GNP 1968 1980 (in 1968 $)	
	1968	1980	1968	1980	1968	1980
	(in millions)		(in 1968 $ billions)		(in 1968 $)	
Argentina	23·6	29·0	15·4	27·7	653	955
Brazil	88·2	123·7	22·1	42·0	251	340
Mexico	47·3	70·6	26·8	57·1	567	809
Venezuela	9·7	14·9	8·5	13·6	876	913
Andean bloc*	52·3	71·6	18·1	32·5	346	454
Total LAFTA†	226·2	315·8	92·7	166·5	410	527
CACM‡	14·0	20·3	4·6	8·7	329	429
Caribbean§	26·2	35·0	12·3	20·9	469	597
Total Latin America	266·3	371·2	109·5	196·9	411	530

* Consisting of Bolivia, Chile, Colombia, Ecuador, and Peru.
† Including Paraguay and Uruguay.
‡ Consisting of Costa Rica, El Salvador, Guatemala, Honduras and Nicaragua.
§ Including Cuba.

The Internal Bottleneck

As mentioned above, the population explosion creates increased capital requirements for social infrastructure and productive investment and simultaneously tends to reduce savings capacity, which is already limited in low-income economies. Inflation and/or political instability in some countries have acted as a further disincentive to savings and investment, encouraging capital flight and discouraging foreign investment. It is significant that the increase in gross domestic fixed capital formation in Latin America – just over 4 per cent annually in 1961–67 – has lagged slightly behind the growth rate of GDP. The Inter-American Development Bank has estimated that in order to attain a 2·5 per cent annual growth in per capita product (which means about 5·5 per cent in GDP), the annual increase in investment outlays must be stepped up to around 6·5 per cent. This would require an increase in total investments from $17·1 billion in 1967 to about $29 billion by 1975 and $40 billion by 1980.

Over 90 per cent of gross regional investment in Latin America is financed from domestic savings. Since the private sector accounts for about 65 per cent on average of domestic capital outlays, the prime task is to stimulate private savings and channel them where they are most needed. But public investments are also essential – particularly in economic and social infrastructure – and they must be financed on a noninflationary basis. An encouraging trend is the growing effectiveness of Latin American governments in mobilizing domestic resources and channelling them into needed public investments. Current revenues of the central government expanded at a faster rate than GDP in 1961–67, and capital outlays rose from 26 per cent to 31 per cent of total central government expenditures.

The most heartening change in Latin America in the past few years is the slower rate of inflation. This is not to say that inflation has been licked. The relative stability attained recently in some countries is still precarious, and others may succumb in the future to the temptation of seeking easy popularity through unrealistic wage increases and deficit-financed public expenditures. However, it is now generally recognized by Latin American governments that inflation is neither an inevitable nor a desirable element in the growth process, and that it can be controlled without sacrificing growth. Where inflation does continue to pose a problem, its worst effects on internal savings and the balance of payments will be minimized through new policies (monetary correction, flexible exchange rates) developed in the 1960s by Chile and Brazil.

The External Bottleneck

The development efforts of most Latin American countries will continue to be hampered by a structural shortage of external resources. Latin America's dependence on foreign financing is twofold:

(1) to supplement the limited supply of investment capital that can be generated through internal savings;

(2) to provide the foreign exchange to pay for necessary imports – especially of machinery and equipment, which now represent about 40 per cent of total imports – and to service the region's existing foreign debt and equity investments. The second aspect represents the more pressing problem for most countries.

73

Because of the unsatisfactory long-term growth of Latin American exports – resulting from the fact that these are still composed mainly of a limited range of primary commodities, many of which face inelastic demand and fluctuating world prices – the region has become increasingly dependent upon capital inflow to balance its international accounts. Almost all Latin countries in recent years have been running deficits on the current account portion of their balance of payments, more or less offset by net inflows on the capital account portion. Such a balance-of-payments structure is not viable in the long run, because the inexorable rise in debt-servicing obligations means that a continuing increase in the gross inflow of new loans and investments is necessary merely to maintain the net inflow unchanged.

To escape from this bind, two things will be necessary:

(1) an increase in the volume and a significant easing in the terms of external financing to Latin America (the greater the easing of terms, the smaller will be the necessary increase in volume); and

(2) successful efforts to expand Latin American export earnings, from both traditional and nontraditional exports (including tourism), and to substitute for third-country imports through greater intraregional trade.

The urgency of the debt-servicing problem, with its close ties to the conditions on which international financing is to be provided in future, is generally recognized today in the capital-exporting nations. There is therefore a good chance that some action will be taken to deal with it, through such measures as a stretch-out of maturities on bilateral aid loans, provision of greater soft-loan funds, through multilateral agencies like the Inter-American Development Bank, or subsidization of interest rates to developing countries. These measures will probably not go as far as the Latin Americans would like, but they will ease the present financial bottleneck to some extent.

The urgency of diversifying exports is also clearly recognized, both in Latin America and abroad. It now appears a reasonable possibility (though by no means a certainty) that some form of tariff preferences for Latin American manufactured and semi-manufactured goods will be introduced within the next few years, either in a worldwide context or on a regional basis with the us.

SOCIAL AND POLITICAL TENSIONS

Latin America is currently in a revolutionary transition from traditional to modern societies, compressing into decades the process that evolved in the northern hemisphere over the past century or more. This period of accelerated change inevitably exerts severe strains on political institutions and social structures that grew out of the circumstances of an earlier age. The roots of violence may be traced still deeper, to the psychological frustration that results from the corrosion of traditional social values and cultural attitudes developed over centuries in a framework of stability that no longer prevails. The traditional Latin American society – agrarian, hierarchical, paternalistic, and family-oriented – involved a whole set of mutually understood rights and obligations (underwritten by religious beliefs) that are incompatible with the increasingly industrial, impersonal, and bureaucratized mass societies that are now emerging.

The common denominator of social unrest in Latin America today is the urgent desire for change. While the proponents of change are everywhere in the ascendancy, they disagree among themselves on everything but the fundamental goal: the building of technologically modern, economically strong, socially just, and politically independent nations. The principal figures in the current social unrest – the students, the revolutionary activists, the progressive wing of the Church, the military, and the impoverished urban masses – are all protagonists of change in this sense.

If governmental stability in a given country is difficult to predict in Latin America, by the same token one of the most predictable things about the region as a whole is its high degree of instability. Since 1960 there have been sixteen successful military coups (compared to eleven in the previous decade) affecting nine of the twenty republics. Ten countries are now governed by military or civilian dictatorship (twice as many as in 1960), and these countries hold 56 per sent of the region's total population. It is safe to predict that the 1970s will witness continued governmental instability with at least one coup per year on average, and that the military will continue to dominate the political scene in a number of countries.

The military leaders of today are less personalistic than their predecessors and more concerned with administrative efficiency and institutional modernization. Their motives for seizing power are

75

principally two: scepticism of their nation's ability to achieve rapid development, which they regard as essential to national pride, and fear of further gains by leftist radicals who, if they ever came to power, might succeed in removing the armed forces from their traditional role as the ultimate arbiter of political conflict in Latin America.

From the viewpoint of foreign investors, there is a crucial distinction between the moderate military reformists, like those in Brazil and Argentina, and the more demagogic variety now in power in Peru and Bolivia. One or the other will probably set the political style for the 1970s in their own and neighbouring countries. Which one will prevail is uncertain at this point.

In the past, Argentina and Brazil have repeatedly pointed the way for major shifts in the continental political scene. But the Peruvian junta's tactic of appealing to mass support through attacks on foreign 'monopolies' and domestic 'reactionaries' has not gone unnoticed by younger and more radical officers in the Argentine and Brazilian military, whose own emphasis on economic stabilization and stimulation of the private sector has failed signally to win them broad popular adherence. If, however, the course being followed in Peru and Bolivia leads to economic stagnation and financial collapse, the surface popularity of these regimes could evaporate swiftly, forcing them either to become more repressive or else take a less radical tack or even abandon power altogether.

NATIONALISM

Rising nationalism is a factor that every company operating in Latin America will have to learn to live with in the future. Increasingly, Latin governments are hedging their hospitality to foreign capital. There is growing concern over the predominance of international companies in taking advantage of regional integration. And the expropriations of us oil companies in Peru and Bolivia, while less typical of the problems faced by investors in manufacturing industries, nevertheless demonstrate that a company that gets on the wrong side of nationalistic forces is bound to lose.

Nationalism in Latin America is a pervasive force, not confined to any one ideological viewpoint or social group. It is expressed by conservatives and leftists alike, and is shared to some degree by businessmen, economists, and government officials, as well as workers, students, and intellectuals. Politicians and government officials often fear that foreign investment leads to economic dependence, particularly on the us, and that the motivations and actions of international companies run counter to the national interest. Local businessmen centre their fears on the threat of competition from giant international firms. Leftist intellectuals are suspicious of both local and foreign capitalists, and antagonistic to the profit move. Rightist intellectuals decry the 'vulgarity' and 'commercialism' of us culture and the business enterprises that spread its seeds abroad. All these work on the man in the street, who is highly susceptible to nationalist arguments and emotions.

Despite the current vogue of the myth that foreign investors are 'decapitalizing' Latin America by remitting more in profits than they bring in fresh capital, most responsible Latins recognize that foreign capital plays an important role in development. However, they are becoming increasingly selective. While some smaller countries still welcome almost any investment that provides foreign exchange and augments scarce local capital, the larger and more developed countries are screening out those that do not offer special benefits such as new technology, export promotion, or local participation. In view of the growing strain on national balances of payments, this selectivity is bound to intensify in the 1970s.

Apart from the alleged burden of profit remittances on the host country's balance of payments, the preoccupations of economic nationalists toward foreign manufacturing investments focus on five points:

(1) The threat of new and injurious competition in industries already occupied by local capital. A number of countries now effectively control this by denying incentive treatment for investments that would duplicate existing ventures. While this often ignores the benefits available from improved technology, it is true that additional competition in a small market is not necessarily healthy even for the newcomer. It would seem wise policy for international companies not to force the issue, especially where openings still exist for new products that might be more profitable.

(2) Fears that established local enterprises will pass into foreign hands, displacing local entrepreneurs. Partly to counter this objection, which is shared even by those most favourably disposed to foreign investment in general, some companies have

77

made it a policy to retain the local owners as partners wherever possible in an acquisition move.

(3) Concern over 'excessive' use of local credit by foreign enterprises. This issue, which is a highly emotional one in many countries, has already led to restrictions of one sort or another in Brazil, Mexico, Peru and Venezuela. A foreign company that invests in Latin America on a shoestring, with the idea of borrowing locally on the strength of parent company or bank guarantees, is inviting trouble for itself and for all other foreign investors.

(4) Fears that regional integration could prove a 'Trojan horse' for foreign investors, enabling them to set up plants in the countries that offer the most liberal investment policies and the richest incentives, and then export freely throughout the region, swamping smaller local competitors. This concern has prompted the Andean Common Market countries to call for an early harmonization of incentives and treatment of foreign capital through their subregion. Mexico has advocated a harder line, within LAFTA, proposing that regional tariff preferences be restricted to goods produced by locally controlled enterprises, but other countries have been understandably cool to this idea, since in practice it would cancel out much of the increased exports they have won through hard-wrung tariff concessions.

(5) Desire for greater local participation and control of foreign investments. The joint venture is still a popular idea with Latin Americans, but many are beginning to realize the difficulties inherent in a marriage between a large international firm and a small local industrialist – particularly if it is a shotgun wedding between two parties who would each prefer at heart to be running his own show. The additional problems posed by multiple joint ventures in an integrating regional market are now widely recognized, and some foreign firms are exploring the possibility of multinational enterprises grouping investors from several Latin countries. While this idea is attractive to Latin Americans, they will generally insist that control of the enterprises rests with the local interest. Another, more dubious variant of the joint-venture concept that is attracting attention today is the 'fade-out formula', whereby the foreign firm has 100 per cent ownership for a certain number of years, at the end of which it must turn over part or all of the enterprise to local shareholders.

Whatever their feelings about such proposals, foreign companies in Latin America will have to come to terms with economic nationalism if their operations are to grow and prosper.

REGIONAL INTEGRATION

Regional economic integration has come to be generally accepted within Latin America – at least in theory – as a necessary condition for continued economic growth and industrial development. The basic reason is that national markets are simply not big enough to support efficient production facilities for many modern industrial products. Particularly for intermediate and capital goods, the only basis on which Latin America can continue its progress in industrialization is through the creation of multinational markets. The adverse balance-of-payments structure described above lends added urgency to the integration effort, since larger and more competitive industries would help to save hard currencies now being spent in imports from outside the area, and in the longer run would help to diversify its own exports into more dynamic product lines.

Despite these powerful economic incentives, and notwithstanding the impressive growth of intraregional trade during the initial years of tariff reductions within the Latin Free Trade Association (LAFTA) and the Central American Common Market (CACM), both integration movements have run into increasing difficulties of late, and their progress will probably be slow.

LAFTA's problems are ultimately political: the reluctance of the 'Big Three' (Argentina, Brazil, and Mexico) to make integration commitments that might involve the surrender of certain industries to other member countries, and the smaller countries' fears of industrial domination by the Big Three. These conflicting national aspirations and interests, combined with the fact that all major decisions of LAFTA are subject to veto by any member country, have blocked the implementation of more effective tariff-cutting procedures and slowed the pace of product-by-product negotiations. As a result, LAFTA has had to postpone from 1973 until 1980 its target date for eliminating tariffs and other barriers on most goods traded among its members. The prospect is that integration within LAFTA as a whole will continue in low gear at least through the mid-1970s, by which time further negotiations are supposed to set the long-range course toward a Latin American Common Market.

In the meantime, national list tariff negotiations and complementation agreements[1] in certain industries will continue to offer opportunities for reduction of tariff barriers on individual products for companies prepared to push their goals through lobbying with national governments and negotiations at industry sectorial meetings.

The brightest hope for accelerated integration within LAFTA in the 1970s now rests with the subregional integration programme worked out by the five countries of the Andean bloc (Bolivia, Chile, Colombia, Ecuador, and Peru). These countries have signed a complex agreement calling for elimination of tariffs among themselves and creation of a subregional common outer tariff by 1980. In order to attract new industries capable of competing with those of the 'Big Three', the Andean countries propose to eliminate trade barriers quickly on a list of products not yet produced within the subregion, and to work out sectorial integration schemes to promote investment in basic or dynamic industries (basic metallurgy, non-metallic minerals, chemicals and petrochemicals, pulp and paper, mechanical products, electrical and electronic products, and food processing). Although Venezuela decided not to sign the Andean agreement at this point, it may join the group later on.

In Central America, the five member countries of CACM have made considerable progress toward integration, achieving intraregional free trade in all but twenty-six items, a common outer tariff on all but twenty, and some progress toward coordination of fiscal policies. The chief problem at present lies in the lingering bitterness created by the brief war between Honduras and El Salvador, which has obstructed the flow of intraregional trade and set back the timetable for new regional projects such as a joint currency-stabilization fund, harmonization of agricultural policies, and standardizing of company laws. Other difficulties centre on CACM's balance-of-payments deficit with the rest of the world, as well as the frictions resulting from the imbalance of intraregional trade, whose ninefold growth since 1961 has heavily favoured Guatemala and El Salvador over the other three countries.

In the coming years CACM must reorient its industrialization policies on more selective lines, placing greater emphasis on industries

[1] National list concessions are tariff reductions granted by individual countries on specific goods imported from any LAFTA country. Complementation agreements establish reductions only among the countries participating in the specific agreement.

that use local rather than imported materials. It will also have to implement the harmonization of investment incentives (theoretically in force since March 1969) which confers preferential conditions on less-developed Honduras.

CHAPTER 5

Assumptions on World Institutional Change

Behind the forecasts in the previous four chapters are several key assumptions about the future. Obviously, it is assumed that there will be no major international armed conflict; there will be no nuclear holocaust. Any predictions about the market of tomorrow require the taking of this assumption. By definition, nuclear holocaust means no future, at least for the northern hemisphere.

Secondly, it is assumed that the belief that the pollution of the earth is irreversible and that man is near destroying his own ecosystem is false. It is true that the pollution situation is far worse than most people believe, and that the effects of increasing pollution are little known. It is also true that little has been done of an effective nature anywhere to counter increasing pollution of air, water, and land. But there is the assumption that serious and effective steps will be made at least to stabilize, if not reverse, the pollution problem in the 1970s and 1980s.

Thirdly, it is assumed that the general breakdown of institutions, and of human thought and value systems, will be reversed through at least the beginnings of the creation of new institutions and values. In other words, an increasing portion of the population of the major markets and of the world will not become alienated; revolutionary aspirations will be answered by evolutionary, but rapid, evolutionary change.

As regards the third assumption, it can be said that man is at least beginning to understand the causes of the situation in which he now finds himself. Stated simply, man was in one stage of development for about 10,000 years, and since 1900 or so has been in another. Until the present century, man was basically a farmer who worked from dawn to dusk and was closely tied to natural phenomena. During this century the centre of man's activity changed from the farm to the crowded city. Working hours and work itself were drastically cut. The electric light totally altered living habits, and man was cut off from nature.

This overwhelming change was accompanied by the phenomenal speed-up of transportation and communications. The earth shrank in size from several months to a few days or several seconds. Until very recently an individual human being knew very little about what happened beyond a few miles from his immediate surroundings; today radio and television mean that man knows a great deal about what is happening everywhere in the world practically as soon as it has happened.

All these crucial events – and more – are summarized in the facile phrase 'the technological revolution'. Technology has changed the world and man drastically, but institutions and values have not as yet changed very much. The central problem today and for years to come is and will be the need to revolutionize institutions and values without destructive crisis and destructive revolution – to make them responsive to post-1900 conditions.

Everywhere is breakdown. The religion of nationalism is challenged just as other religions were challenged in the early stages of the industrial revolution. The nation state, itself a product of the early industrial revolution, no longer enjoys blind worship. But it still provides obstructive forms of thought and deterrents to rational progress.

Governments are in crisis because the constitutions of various countries are no longer relevant to the problems of government. The US constitution, written by farmers, who needed a week or more to travel from their residences to a central point, is only one example of increasing constitutional breakdown.

Many examples, general and specific, of the general breakdown of institutions and values could be cited, but are obviously beyond the scope of this book. However, it should be pointed out that one institution, while in need of rapid change and development, is not in crisis. Indeed, the business corporation seems to be one of the few institutions of the past that is capable of functioning in a more and more effective manner in this century.

In the chapters which follow, various appropriate responses for corporations that wish to continue to function in an increasingly effective manner are suggested. The rest of this chapter concerns itself with one central institutional change that is likely in the next several decades – the reduction in the sovereign power of individual nation states over their national economies and the devolution of powers now vested in the nation state to worldwide, or regional institutions of various types.

THE MONETARY QUESTION

The post-war international monetary system was established at Bretton Woods in 1944 to replace the previous centuries of monetary chaos. In brief, it set up three types of national reserves. The fundamental international reserve unit was to be gold, supplemented by two reserve currencies, the dollar and sterling. In addition, the agreement set forth standards for proper national monetary behaviour, with fixed rates of exchange being the central rule. When a nation faced currency difficulties, it was to receive short-term loans to give it time to 'adjust', i.e. to deflate and reverse its international account deficit.

The Bretton Woods system worked extremely well until the early 1960s. By that time, both of the reserve currencies were no longer accepted as 'as good as gold'. Both the US and the UK were running more or less continual balance-of-payments deficits. Fears of devaluation of one or both or of national actions limiting the convertibility of one or both began to spread. Governments and companies and individuals began to worry about holding these currencies. It was during the 1960s that the Bretton Woods system lost its two reserve currencies.

The second half of the 1960s witnessed a series of international monetary crises of various intensities and lengths. Sterling was under pressure from 1964 until well after it was devalued in 1967. There were brief flights from the dollar into gold every so often. And then in 1968 and 1969 came the crises involving the weakness of the French franc and the strength of the German mark, which was later revalued in 1971.

A host of improvements was grafted onto the Bretton Woods system, the most important of which was a system of intercountry loans of various sorts to help individual central banks to defend their currency's parity.

Three fundamental changes took place in 1968 and 1969. In 1968 the dollar was divorced from gold with the establishment of the two-tier gold system. Probably no one knew at the time how profound a change in the world monetary system was wrought by this action. Its momentous consequences began to be visible only in 1969 when the US dollar rang up its worst balance-of-payments deficit in history, yet owners of dollars decided that holding sterile gold was not as worthwhile as holding dollars on which 10 per cent or so interest rates could be earned. The creation of a new reserve element – the SDRS (Special Drawing Rights) – was the second fundamental change. The third, still unfolding at this writing, is the monetary unification of the European Common Market.

These steps make it possible to state with some confidence that the monetary environment in which international companies will have to operate in the future will be substantially improved. The era of unilateral and substantial devaluation, repeated chaotic conditions in currency markets, and semi-permanent crisis may be ending.

What amounts to a fully new international monetary system seems to be on the horizon. The new system will be far more flexible and will include progress toward both a regional and a more centralized worldwide financial order.

The coming pattern of exchange rates will be determined by basic improvements in several areas.

The 'adjustment process' has proved to be in greatest need of overhaul if realistic exchange rates are to be achieved and maintained over long periods. Reduced to its practical application, this means creation of a mechanism that permits more flexibility in the altering of exchange rates, preferably by a more or less automatic procedure. Fixed exchange parities will remain, but there will be frequent, limited adjustments of them.

Two schemes have been proposed and each one or both together have a very good chance of being adopted.

The 'crawling' or 'creeping peg' is a mechanism for quick adjustment of an exchange rate – downward or upward – when the imbalance in a country's payments becomes obvious. Two methods are possible. One is a controlled peg, i.e. governments free to decide when and to what extent an adjustment should be made, though within limits and at a frequency agreed upon with the IMF.

The other, and generally preferred method, would be a more automatic procedure under which a country must adjust its currency rate when certain changes in payments or trade conditions require it. The difficulty here is establishing the criteria that trigger the change. Factors for such a trigger might include such elements as the domestic rate of inflation, expansion of the domestic money supply, the local interest rate, the balance of trade, capital movement, the balance-of-payments deficit or surplus, etc.

Another mechanism projected is for the exchange rate 'to follow the market' and make official adjustments whenever market pressures require it. But market forces are difficult to control and hard to foresee. Such a trigger would have to separate a legitimate market situation from one caused by speculators. It could lead to warfare in the market place between those wishing to maintain a certain rate of exchange and those wishing to raise or lower it. Even limiting the size and frequency of changes – suggested are changes of 1 per cent or 2 per cent at a time, once or twice a year – would not solve this problem.

The crawling peg in some form will be adopted in one way or the other, although only a restricted number of countries will probably be allowed to apply the system.

The other major proposal that may be adopted in the next few years is a widening of 'trading margins' or 'intervention points': IMF rules have established a one percentage point trading margin for fluctuations above and below the fixed parity (or a 2 per cent total margin); when the limit is reached the central bank must intervene in the market to strengthen or weaken the currency. Most central banks now intervene so as to prevent their currency from being traded at more than 0·75 per cent above or below parity. When intervention cannot be continued even with large borrowings and swap deals, a devaluation becomes unavoidable.

There are proposals to widen the trading margin from 1 per cent on either side of parity to 2–5 per cent, making the total permissible range 4–10 per cent. Too large a widening, however, could create very difficult problems. One of the problems arises from the fact that all currency parities are anchored to the US dollar. Trading between two non-US currencies at cross rates could actually mean doubling the margin. For example, if one currency was traded at 5 per cent above parity against the US dollar and another currency was traded at 5 per cent below, there would be a very unstabilizing 10 per cent difference between the rates of exchange of the two non-US countries. Uncertainty and the resulting need for hedging even short-term trade transactions rule out any widening of the trading margin beyond 2 per cent on either side.

Another unsolved problem is whether wider IMF trading margins should be either mandatory and automatically open to all countries or applied only upon application of individual countries. It is possible that wider margins would be available only on the basis of case-by-case approval by IMF and that the approval could stipulate different margins for different countries.

The monetary system of the 1970s will also be far less constrained by the 'liquidity' problem. Stated simply, liquidity is the sum total of gold and foreign currency reserves held by countries. This figure has been rising much more slowly than has international trade. The result is that most countries have seen their reserves-to-imports ratios getting smaller and smaller, leading to imposition of restrictions on imports (and on capital outflows).

Furthermore, because new gold production was being used for industrial purposes or hoarding, the only way for liquidity to expand was for countries to increase their IMF positions (on which there are very definite limits) or their holdings of foreign currencies, which essentially meant their holdings of dollars. This in turn meant that US balance of payments had to be in more or less perpetual deficit (or intercountry swap operations had to be perpetually expanded).

The liquidity problem may well be solved by the new 'paper gold', the Special Drawing Rights (SDRs), which became available at the beginning of 1970. SDRs are basically accounts created out of thin air, backed by the faith and credit of the IMF's members. They can be used to settle intercountry surpluses and deficits just as gold and dollars are now used. $3·5 billion of SDRs were created in 1970 with provision for $3 billion to be added in each of the two subsequent years. By the end of the 1970s, SDRs could make up the largest proportion of world liquidity. In theory, carefully managed, they could become the only reserve asset at some time in the future. Whatever the result, their creation goes far in solving the world liquidity problem.

Gold will progressively lose its monetary role. The two-tier gold price system has worked, and it looks as if it will continue to work. Sooner rather than later, industrial demand for gold will outrun production and prevent its rebirth as a monetary standard. The one radical method of increasing liquidity vastly, by an increase of the gold price, is no longer expected. Gold as a measure of sound money will soon be dead.

The revision of the monetary system as outlined above is not the ultimate word on the development of a world monetary system. The trend is toward the end of national monetary fragmentation, toward the creation of multicountry or multicurrency blocs, along with more worldwide monetary centralization. The creation of SDRs and increasing of IMF quotas are a visible sign of increasing worldwide (less the communist countries) monetary centralization.

The start toward creation of single regional currencies is the visible sign of the other portion of the trend. 1980 is already the goal for what would amount to a single EEC currency. There would also be what amounts to an EEC central bank.

At a minimum each EEC member will guarantee the parities of each other EEC member currency, and the regular meeting of member country central bank officials will be institutionalized into something permanent and powerful.

What is consequential in this process is not only the evolution of the EEC currency but also the necessity for member countries to give up a substantial portion of their fiscal and monetary powers. For the system to work, there will have to be what amounts to a single EEC budget and business cycle. The cost of money throughout the EEC will have to be the same or very similar. National power over a member's economy will devolve to the new central monetary institution.

Eventually, there will be a central bank organized for Latin American and/or African countries. Finally, the regional central banks will become something like the Federal Reserve banks in the US, but instead of a single currency there would be a number of closely interrelated ones.

This long-term picture will only partially materialize during the 1970s. During this decade, there will still be plenty of currency worries for international corporations. Indeed, the greater flexibility outlined here means considerable flexibility of exchange rates. While a currency may not be changing in as large an amount as in the past, changes are likely to be much more frequent.

WORLD TRADING SYSTEM

One of the reasons that nothing comparable to the reform of the world monetary system has occurred as regards international trade is the very fact that the General Agreement on Tariffs and Trade (GATT) has been so successful in regularizing and controlling national foreign trade policies and in reducing tariffs since its founding in 1947. The need for reform has been less urgent: the world trading system has not broken down as much as has the world monetary system. Indeed the greatest of GATT accomplishments, the Kennedy Round, will not be completed before 1972. However, GATT will need some major streamlining, or it is bound to wither away.

Protectionist forces in many countries are already at work to counter GATT's accomplishments. The possibility that the US will reverse its policies and trade war break out is not out of the question. But this is unlikely.

The early 1970s may be a period dangerously close to a breakdown of international trade, but it is inconceivable to think that mankind is so stupid as to let such a threat continue very long.

What is far more likely is that the 1970s will see further progress, at least on average, toward freer trade among the industrialized countries. A GATT official told a Business International meeting in 1969 what he believed was likely to happen after the completion of the Kennedy Round cuts:

Where duties are nil, consolidating the present duty-free treatment might be examined. Where duties are low, it may be wondered whether such duties are not really more of a nuisance than of real value in many cases, to the extent that they have no significant protective effect, yet simply in many countries are a whole series of formalities that complicate commercial transactions.

For similar reasons, I also feel that thought should be given to the possibility of duty-free admission of tropical products and industrial raw materials into developed countries. In the case of tropical products one would have to resort to interim measures to help certain producing countries, which at present enjoy preferential arrangements, to adjust to the new competition.

Secondly, it would seem to me that, in industrial sectors where technology is very advanced, where the size of producing units is large and production and marketing operations are conducted on a international scale, it would be logical to consider the full abolition of trade barriers.

Otherwise, there is a risk that certain structural problems already apparent may become more serious. For instance, the location of new production units, and their degree of specialization, as well as the organization of distribution channels, might be seriously affected by considerations connected with the sharing of markets.

The speaker concluded that non-tariff barriers to manufactured goods have increased in importance as obstacles to the movement of goods across borders as tariffs have progressively declined. Therefore, GATT should address itself to developing a complete inventory of non-tariff barriers and then establish machinery to deal with them. But he warns that any analysis of non-tariff barriers will discover that many of them will not be of the government type, but be related to business practices that may or may not have anything to do with legality. In other words, the opening of the door to the progressive abolition of non-tariff barriers leads to investigation and abolition of national cartels, among other business practices.

The GATT spokesman also dealt with the agricultural trade problem:

> While great progress has occurred in the reduction of barriers to the international movement of manufactured goods, practically nothing has been done to create a world market in farm products. Rather, the past two decades have seen the world divided up into more and more unviable agricultural markets. Quotas keep products out of the market and raise internal prices. Rising internal prices lead to overproduction. And overproduction leads to export subsidies, which make the international agricultural market an irrational and costly chaos.
>
> In addition, national agricultural support policies cost an ever-increasing amount. They maintain an excessively large farm population when manufacturing is increasingly short of workers. National farm policies raise domestic taxes and prices and limit market growth by keeping workers in jobs of low productivity.
>
> Moreover, if the drawbacks of certain systems of agricultural production are not removed, there is a risk that this burden may increase even more. If the level of guaranteed prices is so fixed as to accommodate marginal or inefficient producers, the result may be a rapid increase in the production of the more efficient farms, which may lead to a tightening of import restrictions, and an increase in the cost of export subsidies. It would seem wiser to envisage limits for the level of guaranteed prices and the volume of production to which these prices apply.

Thus, in spite of the complexity of the social problems that would arise in many industrial countries from a more liberal trend in agricultural policy, it would seem that progress in this area can only be obtained by negotiations bearing not only on import barriers but also on national price and production policies as well as subsidies and surplus disposals.

Liberals will wish to see the issues raised by GATT grappled with, but there is no certainty that the US will propose further tariff cuts on low-tariff and high-technology products, a serious attack on non-tariff barriers, and/or a frontal assault on the stupendous and growing agricultural problem. The International Chamber of Commerce's proposal for a freetrade area for all industrialized countries during the 1970s appears to have no chance at all of realization.

GATT may well have gone as far as it can with its existing statute. It may be that the only way to protect the accomplishments of the past is to hold a new world trade meeting to strengthen GATT itself, but to delay new efforts at dismantling trade barriers.

Dr Gerard Curzon reasons that pressures from the United States and other major trading nations outside the Common Market would require a world trade meeting under GATT auspices to harmonize world patterns of trade and avoid formation of hostile trading blocs.

It is possible that the rump end of Europe may coalesce around a super-Nordek, grouping Finland, Sweden, Norway, Switzerland and Austria, but the pressure for free trade between this group and the enlarged EEC will remain as great as before, and to it will be added pressure which an enlarged EEC would evoke from the United States, Canada and Japan to compensate for the discrimination.

All these various solutions and possibilities point to the same conclusion in the medium-to-long run: a major trade negotiation among all developed countries before 1980.

When Britain enters the Community the United States is likely to be galvanised into action and will ask for negotiating powers from Congress and for compensation from the Community (as is its right under Article XXIV of GATT) for further trade discrimination. In this it will be supported by the Europeans remaining outside the Community, Canada, Japan and perhaps Australia and New Zealand. In such a case trade negotiations would materialise relatively rapidly and would constitute the best possible outcome to all our troubles.

When Britain enters, it will bring only a few other countries with it. The division of Europe will therefore continue, and the pressure thus created will be sufficient to bring the EEC, the rest of Europe and the United States to the negotiating table in GATT. Even if the United Kingdom should turn back at the last this time, there is likely to be a gathering of industrial countries for trade negotiations in GATT because an economically bisected Europe makes no sense to industrialists. We therefore reach the paradoxical conclusion that whatever happens this year, a broadly based trade negotiation of the Kennedy Round type is likely to take place within the decade in order to reduce the discriminating elements of the Community to livable proportions.

A GATT FOR NON-TRADE MATTERS

The success of GATT and IMF, even if limited in many respects, on regularizing and setting standards of national behaviour in matters of national trading and monetary policies has led to increasingly frequent suggestions for establishment of another organization – or possibly widening the powers of the Organization for Economic Cooperation and Development (OECD) – to provide similar regularization and standards for other aspects of national economic policy on international matters.

The various proposals rarely are exactly the same, but they all stem from the increasing need to alter the present jungle of nationally competing, or extraterritorial, or just plain different laws and practices on such matters as anti-trust, trade boycotts, taxation, the issuance of securities, industrial standards, rights of establishment, the movement of capital, etc.

Some of the more radical proponents of such schemes would like to see the establishment of worldwide tax laws or at least harmonization of national tax regimes, at least as they affect other countries and international corporations (for tax laws one can substitute antitrust or patent laws and the like). These radicals would also like to see all actions of an economic nature by one country that may affect the economies of other nations subjected to some sort of review or approval mechanism.

For example, if the US unilaterally limits the amount of funds a US resident tourist may spend outside the US, there would be serious negative consequences in all countries in which US tourist revenue is an important factor in balancing deficit trade positions (e.g. Mexico, some of Europe). Or if the US imposes taxes on loans to foreigners or directly limits them, shouldn't other powers at least have an organized right to respond? Or better shouldn't some sort of limits exist on the travel or capital-limiting nation?

While GATT covers many of the similar types of actions when they concern the movement of goods, there is no GATT for a vast array of other national actions that can be just as harmful to other nation states as import restrictions.

There is not much likelihood of the establishment of one overall international agency to set standards and/or review such national actions. Progress in recent days in international institution building has been almost completely limited to improving the functioning of agencies established during the immediate postwar period. Few new international agencies of this type have been established since this period. And little progress can be expected unless such an agency is established.

There is some likelihood of establishment of new agencies for individual types of national actions. The World Bank's efforts at establishing an office to solve international investment disputes is an example, and it could be expanded and developed.

The problem gets down to the question of whether man in his wisdom is willing to alter his ways of thinking and doing only when he is in the midst of a crisis or when the crisis has already destroyed the basis on which untrammelled behaviour previously occurred.

It is unlikely that the many areas of national economic sovereignty noted above will be limited by international regimes except where they can be grafted onto existing international institutions, unless crisis levels are reached. It is probable that new international agencies will be established for pollution (the world's air is the world's air) and for the preservation and development of the oceans. The alternative to international regimes in these two matters is so catastrophic that even slow-changing establishments will have to respond.

There cannot help but be a continuous and (in historical perspective) rapid withering away of national sovereignty during the near future, but the withering will be sufficiently slow to assure that the world will continue to have plenty of crises and near-crises to keep newspaper columns full.

For every real and practical step in the fading of national sovereignty there will be counteractions from nations in a desperate effort to fight with the future. Nationstates are not disappearing. Indeed, it is quite conceivable that the optimistic picture of economic expansion (and of world peace) presented here will be overwhelmed by the insistence of nations that no world is better than a world in which man is governed by the philosophy of the greatest good for the greatest number – regardless of national boundaries.

HELPING THE LESS DEVELOPED

The very essence of GATT – the concept of the most-favoured-nation – is under severe stress, with the attack led not only by the conservative protectionists, but rather by the radicals. The proposal – now supported by the US government with textiles and shoes excepted – to have industralized countries provide tariff preferences for goods manufactured in less developed countries could materialize in the early 1970s.

The institution of a tariff preference system of this type may be of great help to some international corporations. Firms may find it advantageous to transfer production of certain products to less developed countries for sale to other units of the company in industralized countries. IBM, Facit, and Burroughs have already done this to one degree or another, without tariff preferences.

The proposal for industrialized country tariff preferences for the less developed is one of the few new ideas that appeared in the foreign assistance area during the 1960s. What was to be a development decade turned out to be the decade in which the foreign aid programmes of many of the rich nations, particularly of the US, became progressively more miserly.

Of course, there were many non-industrialized countries that developed rapidly during the decade and there were a number of aid givers that sharply increased their aid flows, but there was also a growing disenchantment with the techniques of foreign aid. And there was growing recognition that aid loans were becoming an

94

albatross around the necks of the aid receivers. Each year the amount of funds necessary to service foreign debt grew greater and greater, eating up every increase in export earnings.

The scheme of preferences is aimed at the concept of trade, not aid: if the poor country could export, it could pay for the capital goods, raw materials, and technological and managerial services that it needed to develop its own economy. Thus, the tariff preference concept is parallel to another new idea of the 1960s – the concept of expansion of exporting industries in the non-industrialized countries rather than the expansion of import substitution industries.

Given the rising domestic pressures on most of the industrialized countries, it is unlikely that the flow of foreign aid in the 1970s will rise any faster than it did during the 1960s, even with Japan increasing its aid flows substantially. It does not appear that the multilateral aid flow will continue to increase but will instead remain a comparatively minor portion. And aid grants and loans will probably continue to be tied, by and large, to procurement of goods and services in the aid-giving country.

The 1970s will probably see continuance of the greater reliance on private investment rather than government-to-government flows. This means more countries will create investment guarantee programmes, and the existing programmes may be improved. The World Bank's investment arbitration programme will probably be made more useful as well.

In sum, one of the world's most serious problems – the gap in incomes between the peoples of the industrialized countries and those of the non-industrialized – will continue to occur. Indeed the gap will probably continue to widen, except for a few exceptional areas.

The widening gap presents a serious possibility of eventual armed confrontation between the rich and the poor, the powerful and the weak. It also presents a case of massive lost opportunity for the improvement of the standards of living of all mankind.

If economic growth could be greatly speeded in the poor countries, a substantial portion of the additional wealth created in the world would spread beyond the borders of the underdeveloped world. If per capita imports of a market like India could be raised ten times, international corporations, workers, and everybody else outside India would be better off. Perhaps, the rapid development of the poor countries will some day become the great new frontier of world business growth. But such a possibility is many years away.

CHAPTER 6

Meeting Corporate Financial Needs

One other aspect of tomorrow's business environment must at least be touched upon because of its critical importance. While there is great probability of a much stronger, more realistic, and more flexible international monetary system during the 1970s, there is also almost a certainty that the 1970s will witness an intensification of the capital shortage that has been progressively worsening during the past several decades. The growth rates forecast in this present study will be achieved only if enough capital can be found so that corporations can take advantage of solid growth opportunities and governments can meet the rapidly rising demand for social investment in cities, housing, transportation, health, education, and anti-pollution.

The corporation almost everywhere has seen its capital requirements rising, and its net worth, as a percentage of total assets, falling. A few years ago US companies on average had equity equal to about three-quarters of total assets, net working capital at more than double current liabilities, and new projects were often totally self-financed. There has been a steady fall in all these ratios. Self-financing ratios of European companies have also been falling quite rapidly during the past decade. Corporations have much smaller relative cash positions than they had ten years ago. Major firms such as the Penn Central have found themselves in such capital-short positions that they have had to go bankrupt.

These indicators are all signs of the intensifying capital shortage, and of the major shift in corporate borrowing from short- to medium- and long-term financing. They represent the financial results of the rapidity of change that technology has caused, of the need to increase the ratio of machinery to ever more expensive labour, of the faster obsolescence of fixed capital, of increasing expenditures on R & D and in-house training programmes, of

96

rising corporate tax rates, and of just plain increase in population.

While corporate tax rates may not be rising much during the 1970s, neither is there much likelihood that they will come down. And there is every likelihood that the other factors tightening cash positions will be getting even stronger. The rate of technological change will be faster during the 1970s than during the 1960s. Obsolescence of machinery will probably continue to occur faster than in the past. Wage rates and fringe costs will be rising more rapidly and the need to find funds to purchase more efficient machinery will increase. The need to invest in R & D and in internal training is also fast expanding. Add to these the costs of antipollution equipment and of finding substitutes for materials which the world will be running out of in the next decades.

The general phenomenon of bigger and bigger government investment in social capital is also unlikely to reverse itself over the decade as a whole. Governments will continue to siphon off huge percentages of available savings in every major world market. More people in the 1970s will be in the unproductive young and retired age groups.

In sum, demand for money will be growing faster in the 1970s than in the 1960s. Unfortunately, there does not seem to be any great likelihood that savings, and therefore the supply of funds for lending, will grow more rapidly than in the past. And it is fairly certain that prices in most countries will be inflating at a faster rate than was the case during the past decade which will militate against money creation by central banks.

The obvious conclusion is that the long-term trend toward higher interest rates will continue. Bluechip companies paid 10 per cent or more for borrowings during 1969. They will probably be paying as much or more at various times during the present decade.

Of course, interest rates will fall from the 1969–70 levels for various periods during the 1970s. Best borrowing rates in various countries might be 3–4 percentage points below the 1969–70 highs in the 1970s, but they will probably also rise above the 1969–70 records in the mid-1970s and again at the end of the decade.

At Business International's first long-range planning roundtable in the early 1960s, it was predicted that interest rates would by 1980 be more or less the same in every major market of the world. This prediction has already almost come true.

The Eurodollar market has become the great equalizer. What

happens is that, for domestic anti-inflationary reasons, the US pushes up interest rates. This increase immediately occurs in the Eurodollar market as US banks and business borrow Eurodollars to replace more costly (or unavailable) domestic dollars. Higher interest rates in the Eurodollar market attract funds from other investors, most notably Europeans, who convert local currency deposits into Eurodollar deposits to earn higher yields. In order to stem outflows from local markets, European central banks boost their local interest rates.

While some differences in interest rates remain between the US and Europe and among European countries, the range of the differences has narrowed. With the mechanism of the Eurodollar market interrelating US and European rates and with financial officers learning to secure funds at the least expensive place they can find in the world rather than automatically in their domestic markets, what differences still remain in national interest rates will disappear more or less completely during the 1970s.

Corporate financial officers became very important people toward the end of the past decade. They not only had to become magicians, finding new ways to locate available money and getting lenders to provide it to their keep, they also had to protect corporate assets located in the many countries in which threats of devaluation existed.

In the 1970s financial officers will become even more important corporate executives. While the nature of devaluation threats will be different, they may become more continuously consequential to corporate profit results. Corporate hedging operations increased in frequency and consequence during the second half of the 1960s. They will become even more frequent and more consequential with a more flexible international financial system.

And the ability of the financial officer to have enough funds in hand or on call when needed for new profitable projects, for normal expansion, and for new machinery will be even more crucial to a company's profitability than in the past. The financial officer will have to be a worldwide expert, knowing the sources and techniques of borrowing wherever in the world funds are available. He will have to be at least as ingenious as he was during the past few years in plotting new methods of enticing funds from individuals and institutions that have them. And he will have to become more adept at investing short-term excess corporate cash so that the higher cost of borrowing is at least partially offset by higher interest income.

SELF-FINANCING

The single most important source of funds for a company is within itself. The 1970s will no doubt witness a marked rise in the sophistication of corporations in self-financing techniques. Self-financing generally has provided 70–100 per cent of the financial needs of companies in the past. There are basically two ways to improve this percentage: cutting down on capital requirements; and increasing the amount of internally generated funds. The very fact of improved internal financing makes it easier for a corporation to borrow external funds.

One of the best ways to avoid capital shortages is to take better long-term investment decisions. There is far greater urgency today than in the past for managers to build plants that are the right size for the market. In the old days, a conservative manager generally attempted to determine proper plant size through a cursory market forecast and then added a certain percentage to the plant capacity figure to make sure no serious production shortages might develop.

Such seat-of-the-pants management is no longer wise. More thorough market forecasts are needed, as well as more definite determinations of plant capacity. Excess capacity will be one of the most unforgivable business sins of the future. Nothing ties up expensive capital quite so much (except perhaps technological failure to get or keep a plant operating) as excess capacity.

Similarly, worldwide production of components and multisourcing of components and raw materials are techniques that can play a consequential part in the long-term self-financing area. Multisourcing possibilities reduce the horrendous effect of local strikes and plant closedowns because of shortages of materials.

Another technique of major consequence is corporate utilization of modern communication, transportation, and teleprocessing (as well as computers) systems to improve inventory management so that the funds tied up in inventory can be greatly reduced. Inventory control and management on a Europewide basis (or at least EEC-wide) is simply common sense, just as it has been common practice on a US-wide basis for decades.

One method now being developed by US-domiciled companies

to alleviate the financial pressures limiting the scope for corporate expansion is the treatment of cash flow on a worldwide (or at least US and European) consolidated basis. Corporations are learning to reduce their need for external borrowing and thus cut the costs of borrowing by shifting funds not being well used by one national unit of the company to other units that are in need of funds. And they are learning to increase their income from investing short-term cash availabilities at highest possible yield and greatest safety.

In sum, companies are developing systems of international cash management, just as they once did the same thing within the home country markets. Sophisticated companies are now aware, to the degree possible, that they should be operating their business, as if no national borders existed. The crises and the increasing difficulty of securing funds and their ever-rising cost have been catalysts to make managers attempt to operate more sensibly in the emerging world market.

While national borders – and with them varying currency controls, varying tax systems, rates, and patterns, and varying exchange risks – still exist, and will no doubt be around for a long time to come, it is a manager's job to operate in the most rational and profitable manner possible. Therefore, sophisticated companies are paying close attention to the real effects of national differences, but are ridding themselves of the psychological 'effect' of national boundaries. As a key executive of a very large US company put it: 'We are operating as if the world were organized the way it ought to be.'

Internationalizing cash management, within the real considerations of national currency and tax laws, is simply another way to do something better, to reduce waste and duplication, to cut costs and boost profits.

EXTERNAL FINANCING

The trend toward less short-term financing and more medium- and long-term external financing will continue during the 1970s. The basic reason for the trend is that short-term funds are largely the province of the commercial banks, and the commercial banks are the one set of financial institutions well controlled by the central banks. Whenever central banks embark on a policy to restrain inflation, they hit the commercial banks and short-term credits.

Until a few years ago central bankers struck at short-term credit through higher interest rates. Now it is not uncommon to use another weapon: actual limitations on the amount of short-term credit a bank may provide. This tool may well spread during the 1970s. And credit rationing is likely to come into greater use as well. Under credit rationing the central banks control what portions of the short-term credit a bank may lend for different purposes.

Another likely development in the 1970s is the intensification of a trend away from overdrafts in Europe. Central banks are particularly concerned by overdrafts that are never repaid, and may in effect be long-term loans, used by borrowers for fixed-asset investment. Many European central banks are now investigating current overdraft practices, and the US term or demand loan may become more common – possibly even with the US compensating balances, although these are under heavy challenge in the US. At least, there may be moves to force annual repayments of overdrafts. Such developments will make short-term borrowing even less attractive to borrowers in Europe than it is today.

The switch to term and demand loans will be one of many ways in which the borrowing practices on different local credit markets will tend to harmonize as time passes. But this aspect of international harmonization will be far slower than the harmonization of interest rates noted above, at least as regards short-term credit.

The squeeze on existing forms of short-term credit will lead to efforts to develop new forms of short-term credit extension. Commercial banks will not only act as full financial intermediaries, but will also become partial intermediaries to one degree or another. Instead of, in the main, receiving deposits from one set of people and lending them out to another, they will more and more become brokers, putting lenders and borrowers together and arranging a deal for a fee.

This will begin to develop even in short-term credit. One form of this type of brokering may include inter-company loans. Although not now on the horizon, another form may be the development of the commercial paper market, as it is known in the US, in which firms sell short-term paper to lenders at a discount via a financial institution.

The forms of short-term credit are likely to multiply in other ways. In countries where overdrafts are the dominant method of extending short-term credit, discounting of trade bills is likely to increase. Factoring is already increasing in Europe in certain industries. By 1980, there may not be as much short-term credit as corporate borrowers would like, but there will be more ways of borrowing what there is at different rates of interest and different real costs than there is today.

While national markets are expected to maintain a good many local peculiarities during the present decade, conditions and techniques for borrowing medium- and long-term funds are likely to become very similar worldwide. Indeed, through the agency of the Eurodollar market, medium- and long-term lending has already developed a consistency and similarity that would have been considered amazing only a few years ago. Almost all the world's major banks, other than Chase and First National City and those in Japan, have joined into multibank, multicountry medium-term lending institutions, which lend along similar lines. While national medium- and long-term markets will continue to exist, they will assume less and less importance in relation to the international market.

Medium-term today generally means a financing with a maturity of ten or fewer years, although some consider any term over seven or so a long-term loan. An exact definition is not necessary because medium-term generally indicates types of borrowing as well as length of term. The main types are loans or notes to finance purchase of equipment or to bridge the period until long-term financing through equity or debentures is possible.

Today (and tomorrow more so) the main source of medium-term funds everywhere is the Eurodollar market. In this, the commercial banks have already become brokers of money. They sign a loan agreement and as notice is given that money is to be drawn, the banks go out and find the funds on the Eurodollar market.

The main form of medium-term funds today (and tomorrow more so) is the revolving credit, under which the borrower receives money over a short period and repays over a longer period. Typically, the borrower may draw the loan over three years, and repay over five, both from the date of the signing of the agreement.

Today the interest rate of the loan is established at the date of each drawing for a 90- or 180-day period. The rate is reset at each subsequent 90- to 180-day period. The rate is usually some portion of a percentage point over the interbank Eurodollar rate for 90- or 180-day funds on the day of the drawing or resetting of the rate.

The bank from which the borrower borrows is simply a broker, collecting a fee.

Borrowing corporations, of course, would like to borrow medium-term at a fixed interest rate, but it is unlikely that their wishes will be heeded. It is conceivable that some borrowers will be able to negotiate maximums on the floating interest rate (the banks would insist on minimums, too, in such a case). But the beating that financial institutions have taken with fixed rates in the recent past will not be forgotten very soon.

What is likely is the development of more 'deal type' borrowings, in which the borrower provides sweeteners such as warrants, stock options, or other equity 'kickers' to the lender. In such cases, it is probable that lenders will agree to fixed interest rate charges, or at least to maximum or fixed rates for longer than 90–180 days. Loans of this type have already been negotiated, and are likely to become more common.

It may be that the floating rate base will be changed to something other than the Eurodollar rate or to a combination of rates. Either one or a combination of the Eurodollar rate, federal funds rate, or the US commercial paper rate may be used.

The only type of medium-term loan that is likely to carry fixed interest rates (other than loans carrying sweeteners and certain debenture-like notes) will be export credit. Export credit has been the favoured financing area for some time. Governments have vied with each other as to which could have the easiest and most subsidized export credit programme. Today, firms can buy equipment across borders on five-year terms at 6 per cent or so. Such loans are one of the biggest business bargains available today.

These bargains will continue during the 1970s, although the differentials between the subsidized export finance rate and normal rates may narrow, at least during periods when normal rates are low. However, even if the rate differential were to be eliminated, export credit is generally easily available in most exporting countries even during the most stringent of money squeezes.

What has been said for medium-term funds can in essence be repeated for long-term borrowings, although the international long-term market will not as completely overwhelm the national long-term markets as will be the case for medium-term. The difference is government financing. Local governments will work hard to maintain long-term markets so that they will be able to continue to spend more than they can obtain in tax revenues and be able to refinance past borrowings. Local tax laws will also help maintain local long-term markets.

The most obvious local market that will survive as a separate and independent entity will be the US debenture market, but it will largely be limited to fund raising for uses within the US. While there is some hope that the Foreign Direct Investment Programme will be greatly eased in the 1970s, it is doubtful that the US interest equalization tax will be removed for quite some time. Furthermore, some restraints on US corporate investors abroad are likely to remain for the foreseeable future.

Local, special markets will also remain and be useful places to finance under various national incentive programmes. These programmes have become more and more advantageous as capital has become more and more scarce. Indeed, the cheapest long-term money in the world today is available in several European countries (10–15 years at several percentage points below normal domestic rates) if a corporation will invest in a plant in specified areas where there is widespread unemployment. The sweetness of the terms of these loans may be lessened, but the direction still is for expansion of these programmes. It may be that new forms of financial incentives (e.g. highly favourable lease-back terms) will be available in some countries in the 1970s.

As to the main source of long-term money, the Eurobond, the brief history of the market indicates that improvisation will be the key element. The market itself and the techniques used so far were invented by ingenious corporate treasurers and underwriters. And ingenious corporate treasurers will invent the techniques of the future, aided by the international underwriting community.

As with medium-term borrowing, the sweetener has become the central question. The first Eurobonds were straight debentures with the improvisation directed toward reducing currency risks for the lender. Then came the convertible debenture wave, which lost much of its steam when the New York Stock Market went to pieces in 1969. Now detachable warrants are becoming more common.

It is impossible to predict what improvisations will be coming next or over the full 1970s, but improvisations there will be. Terms will be shorter at various times. Convertibility premiums may get narrower or wider. A corporation may combine convertibility and warrants. Unit-of-account borrowings may increase as exchange rules change more frequently. Or some less complex system will be devised to protect the bond-buyer from currency exchange risks.

There are some clouds on the Eurobond horizon. One is the consistency of data on the corporation provided in the prospectus of Eurobond issues. The early issues were all accompanied with a prospectus that met the standards required by the US Securities and Exchange Commission. But there is no legal requirement for any prospectus at all.

The Eurobond market is policed by the underwriters, who agree to float an issue or refuse to do so. The underwriters may be lax in insisting on a decent prospectus or they can insist on it. What will probably happen one of these days is that one of the Eurobond issues will turn sour.

If the issue is one in which no decent prospectus was issued, then some sort of prospectus-policing mechanism will be created. It is conceivable that this will be an IATA-like agency, drawing together all the main underwriters and establishing common rules, just as the international airlines do. It is also conceivable that EEC will establish some sort of SEC for any securities sold on the EEC markets.

Another cloud is the low efficiency of the secondary market for Eurobonds. It is difficult and time-consuming for an investor in a Eurobond to sell it to another investor. While daily quotes are published and the bonds are listed on one or more exchanges, the secondary market is very poorly organized. It can take up to three months to get one's money.

As the total number of Eurobonds on the market increases, the need for an efficient secondary market will magnify. It is quite conceivable that the failure to develop an adequate secondary market will put a limit on the amount of Eurobonds that can be floated.

Another cloud is the tax evasion factor. Eurobonds are bearer securities purchased for an investor by a bank in another country. The interest earnings are credited in the other country, and it is apparently not customary for the investor to include the interest on his annual tax return.

Again, as the Eurobond market grows in volume, local tax authorities are bound to become more and more curious, if not downright unhappy, about a bond market so obviously attuned to tax evasion.

It is very much in the interest of international corporations to assist in removing or at least mitigating these three problems. Everyone agrees that, barring the clouds just mentioned, the Eurodollar market and Eurobonds in their various forms, terms, and currencies will continue to grow during the 1970s.

INTERNATIONAL EQUITY FINANCING

There has been almost a complete lack of equity financing by international corporations except in their home market. There have been a few attempts to internationalize equity issues. Solvay, for instance, went public in November 1967 by using the underwriting and selling technique developed in the Eurobond market. And a few similar issues have followed, mainly by Japanese companies. European banks have occasionally also sold some portion of US domestic issues to their own customers in Europe. But none of these attempts comes close to the size and regularity of the Eurobond market.

There are a great many reasons for this lack of international equity financing, ranging from the ease with which Europeans can purchase US (or other) shares on the domestic market and individual national tax complexities to differences in the way Europeans and Americans invest, and selling commissions two or three times higher in Europe than in the US. While European and Japanese companies may follow the Eurobond route and sell 'Euroequity', it is doubtful that many US-domiciled firms, if any, will do so until a good many of the present impediments are cleared away.

Of course, there have been equity-like sales in the convertible Eurobond issues, but early evidence indicates that the convertibility feature is being used by investors only as a hedge. Eurobond investors are converting into equity as a transition mechanism, when it is profitable to do so, as a method of switching out of the early low-interest Euroconvertibles. The investor converts, sells the stock and invests in higher-yielding convertibles.

What appears to be a fruitful area for semi-equity financing is not on the Eurobond market, but on domestic European markets. In this situation, the international company sells debentures, with conversion rights to parent equity, on the local market to local residents for local currency. Several US firms have done this in the UK and Belgium. This route is reputed to create goodwill with the local government (the funds raised are used within the country) and to develop favourable publicity for the issuing company.

Today, a corporate treasurer has many choices for raising medium- and long-term funds for international use. Taking Belgium as an example, he could secure term loans in Belgian francs of up to twelve years in amounts of $10 20 million, possibly more. He could place up to twenty-year bonds in smaller amounts with local institutional investors. He could secure a revolving loan of five to seven years in any of the leading Eurocurrencies. He could issue straight bonds denominated in dollars, Deutschemarks, or units of account. Or he could raise substantial amounts by issuing convertible debentures.

As noted regarding short-term credit, the ways in which funds will be securable will increase in number during the 1970s, keeping in mind that the various factors that make up each method will be aimed at enticing the investor to invest in your company rather than somebody else's. The company that develops its internal self-financing systems best and becomes the most sophisticated and ingenious in financial matters will not have major difficulties finding the funds it needs during the 1970s.

PART TWO

CENTRAL RESPONSES FOR CORPORATE SURVIVAL

Introduction

The 1970s will be years of great challenge and great opportunity
for every corporation. But the opportunities will at best be only
partially grasped and the challenges may overwhelm, unless the
corporation responds internally, utilizing the new techniques that
are being developed by the more advanced business theoreticians
and corporations of the world.

It is clear that the 1970s will be an even more competitive decade
than were the 1950s and 1960s. National borders are becoming
still less and less a hurdle for the free movement of goods, capital,
ideas. National authorities and regional commissions are expanding
their attack on what they construe as monopolistic practices in
various forms. And technological change may be slowing down in
some sectors, but it is speeding up in others – bringing new competition for the corporation that thinks it may sit on its laurels and
its market share and profits.

The four commentators' responses presented in this section are,
of course, only four of a much wider range of techniques, methods,
and programmes that companies might adapt to prepare themselves
for the competitive battles of today and tomorrow. They are,
however, four of the most crucial areas for internal innovation. As
well, they are four areas where competitive firms are likely to be
taking actions that could leave those companies failing to adapt
far behind in the race for survival.

CHAPTER 7

Perlmutter and the Geo-Centric Imperative

Howard Perlmutter's main area of analysis is the development of techniques that today's corporations may adopt in order to survive in the emerging single world market. Perlmutter assumes that the speed at which national markets have been integrating economically will accelerate, that companies failing to change their own attitudes and structures at an accelerating pace will lose out in sales and profits to those that do.

While Perlmutter is not the originator of the idea that by 1985 about 300 firms will produce half the world's industrial production, he often cites this figure. He describes the successful companies of 1985 as of two types: the super-giants (or 'megafirms') and the little fishes. The super-giants are the huge companies, say between 200 and 400 of them, that are the great manufacturers worldwide; the little fishes are the small firms who enjoy the advantages of specialization, of great speed of decision making, and of adaptability because of their size and closeness to customer needs.

The medium-sized firm, for Perlmutter, is ticketed for a very hard future. For they will enjoy neither the advantages of the super-giants nor of the little fishes.

THE SIX ADVANTAGES OF THE SUPER-GIANT

Perlmutter cites six factors that will give the worldwide super-giants significant competitive advantages over their medium-sized and geographically limited competitors:

(1) Super-giant international firms will find it easier to get capital. They will generate more earnings, and constitute less risk for bankers, financiers, and shareholders. These firms can risk sustaining larger losses and still survive. Even today General Electric is purported to have invested $200 million thus far in its

unprofitable venture into the computer business with Machines Bull, but the corporation still reports profits as a business totality.

(2) Super-giant international firms will be able to diversify, replace obsolescent products rapidly, and still maintain worldwide production and distribution of all their products in both developing and developed countries. They will be seen as reliable and trustworthy on the global scale.

(3) Super-giant international firms can maintain a high level of research in such advanced areas as energy, food, and space technology, data processing, aircraft, electronics. As an example, IBM is reputed to have invested in the neighbourhood of $5 billion over four years to develop the 'hardware' for the 360 series of computers.

(4) Such firms have the resources to acquire the middle-sized national or regional firms and offer them worldwide markets for their products, whereas the middle-sized firm simply cannot afford to build up a manufacturing and marketing function worldwide, except in a very narrow product range.

(5) The super-giant firms can afford to hire the best specialists and managers in the world to carry out the worldwide line and staff functions in marketing and manufacturing, in research and development, in personnel, in legal matters, and in finance.

(6) Senior managers are committed to these goals. Perlmutter notes the self-fulfilling prophecy wherein senior managers plan as if the concentration process were inevitable, thus accelerating it. Perlmutter believes there are no significant forces in the world opposing the super-giants. He dismisses consumers and trade unions as effective countervailing forces. He admits the nation state as a powerful potentially hostile force, but refuses to join those who forecast a serious confrontation between emerging worldwide corporation and nation state. Rather he feels that nation states and corporations have too much to lose in confrontation and a great deal to gain from cooperation. Hence he optimistically concludes that the potential adversaries will avoid a collision course. Indeed, one of his prescriptions for the corporation that will survive requires the ability to develop partnerships with most, if not all, nation states.

To understand how to survive the internationalization process, one must comprehend the way corporations are structured today. For Perlmutter the key element of structure is not how product, function, and geography are formally interrelated in the corporate organization chart. Rather it is the central attitudinal core of a corporation's top management, which becomes the central attitudinal core of all key managers within the corporation.

THE ETHNOCENTRIC FIRM

In general all companies with significant operations in markets beyond the borders in which they are domiciled today fall into two general attitudinal types: ethnocentric or polycentric. The ethnocentric firm is one in which the main attitude, revealed in executive actions and experienced by foreign subsidiary managers, is: 'We, the home country nationals, are superior to, more trustworthy and more reliable than, any foreigners in headquarters or subsidiaries.'

The ethnocentric firm has most of its top management and corporate staff centred in the home country. Its domestic home country organization is complex; its foreign organization is generally simple, with limited staff support functions located outside the home country.

The ethnocentric firm reserves most of the key decisions to domestic corporate headquarters. It is highly centralized. There is a high volume of reports from the foreign subsidiaries to the centre. What comes from the centre to the subsidiaries are largely one-sided orders, commands, and advice.

The ethnocentric firm applies home standards to evaluate people and performance. Rewards and incentives are far higher in headquarters than in the foreign subsidiaries. Its recruiting and development policies are those of the home country and the main drive is to develop nationals of the home country to fill all key positions throughout the world. The ethnocentric firm identifies itself with the home country wherever it operates.

THE POLYCENTRIC FIRM

The polycentric firm takes a route opposite to that of the ethnocentric firm. Its basic approach is: 'Let the Romans do it their way, since we really don't understand the local market and local

115

ways of doing business'. While most US-based companies tend to fall into the ethnocentric mould, most European-based firms tend to follow the polycentric design.

The polycentric firm has a highly varied organizational pattern, with foreign operations often highly independent of domestic operations. Worldwide headquarters has relatively little authority over foreign operations and makes few decisions for the managers of the foreign subsidiaries. There is relatively little communication between headquarters and the foreign subsidiaries.

The polycentric firm does not attempt to universalize domestic evaluation and control techniques, nor does it follow consistent reward and incentive patterns. Generally, foreign subsidiary staff is totally local in national origin, or it may include nationals of the home country, but these men are usually located in the foreign subsidiary for their whole careers. The polycentric firm emphasizes identification with each of the countries in which it operates, and de-emphasizes the connection with home country. Besides the localization of staff the local corporate name is often different from that of the parent.

In a sense, the polycentric approach is like that of a holding company that wishes to enjoy a substantial piece of every national market, but the interrelationship of the holding company and each national operating unit is only financial. The holding company has a portfolio, rather than management investment, relationship with the subsidiaries.

Some of the Weaknesses

The stylized description of these two attitudinal structures helps to make it easy to see what is wrong with each of the forms. The ethnocentric attitude is basically imperialism in another form. The key element as regards advancement in the company – and because the ethnocentric attitude dominates top management, indeed all management – is the happenstance of where someone is born. It is not a man's capabilities and performance.

While many ethnocentric companies aver that they fill each job with the best man available, this sort of statement is normally a total self-delusion. Admittedly, a few foreigners do make the grade into senior corporate positions. A few even make it into the top management of a company. But these men are the rare exceptions, who have become Americanized (or Frenchified or Germanized) pretty totally during their career with the ethnocentric company.

The greatest single weakness of the ethnocentric company is that it places in front of itself a great obstacle in accumulating what many believe is the single most important corporate resource – capable managers. The ethnocentric firm cannot possibly recruit and hold the best men outside the border of their home country. Perforce, they cannot attract and keep those with high ambitions, for the best people will not want to work for a company that by nature limits their advancement, or a company in which they are second-class citizens.

It may be true that the American culture, mentality, and educational system does produce more managers than any other (although this is highly debatable), but an American ethnocentric company limits its possibility of accumulating good managers to just 6 per cent of the world population. Even if America produces four times as many managers as the average country, the America ethnocentric firm is cutting itself off from many of its potential management sources.

There are other things wrong with the ethnocentric approach, ranging from over-identification with the political actions of the home country to an inability to adapt rapidly to both change and different conditions in the markets outside the home country, but space does not permit their coverage here.

The polycentric approach is perhaps just as self-restrictive as the ethnocentric. It, too, has its second-class citizens, but of a different form. More consequential is the inability of the polycentric firm to adapt to the integration of national economies. Because the polycentric company is so decentralized, its subsidiaries – as economies integrate – begin to compete with each other. There is no central headquarters to create rational worldwide responses to emerging worldwide markets. And duplication among the headquarters and growing national operations becomes rampant – and expensive.

THE GEOCENTRIC FIRM

Without the benefit of Perlmutter's analysis and his strong ethnocentric and polycentric approaches we have already begun to see the problems that either approach creates. The realities of corporate life are breaking down ethnocentrism and polycentrism. They will

117

break them down much more as the single world market emerges in the coming decades.

Perlmutter's geocentric approach calls for corporations to become world-oriented. As one worldwide company puts it: 'We want to Unileverize our Indians and Indianize our Unileverans.' Under the geocentric approach, there are no second-class citizens: the best man, regardless of nationality, is chosen for each post. The whole world is searched, not only for markets and materials, but also for ideas, standards of behaviour and ways of doing business, for places to build plants, and conduct R & D, and for people. The ultimate in the geocentric approach is elimination of nationalistic prejudices, and creation of a concept of the earth as a single spaceship.

The geocentric firm would have totally worldwide integrated structure, with each unit interdependent on each other unit. While there certainly would be a single worldwide headquarters, its location or the location of a management subofficer would be in accordance with the best place to locate rather than necessarily in the country in which the parent company is legally domiciled. And its orders, commands, and advice would be determined on the basis of a collaborationist approach. Heads of national subsidiaries would be a vital element in the decision-making process.

The geocentric firm would create a mixture of both universal and local standards of evaluation and control. Managers would be rewarded for reaching a combination of worldwide and local (or divisional) goals. Performance and contribution to the firm's objectives would be the basis for promotion. Identification would be both with worldwide corporate and local national interests. Recruitment, training, and development would be based on staffing of all jobs without prejudice to one's birthplace.

The Geocentric Will Survive

It is Perlmutter's belief that the 200–400 firms that will be the super-giants of tomorrow will be those companies that become geocentric in approach. Perlmutter admits that it is not easy to become geocentric. It is a slow, painful process requiring the firm to overcome a wide variety of obstacles that result in the main from the fact that the world itself is in a slow, painful, but irreversible emergence into a single marketplace.

Perlmutter lists seventeen factors that force the firm toward geocentrism (eight external and nine internal). They are:

External	Internal
1. Technological and managerial know-how increasing in availability in different countries	1. Desire to use human vs. material resources optimally
2. International customers	2. Observed lowering of morale in affiliates of an ethnocentric company
3. Local customers' demand for best product at fair price	3. Evidence of waste and duplication in polycentrism
4. Host country's desire to increase balance of payments	4. Increasing awareness and respect for good men of other than home nationality
5. Growing world markets	5. Risk diversification in having a worldwide production and distribution system
6. Global competition among international firms for scarce human and material resources	6. Need for recruitment of good men on a worldwide basis
7. Major advances in integration of international transport and telecommunications	7. Need for worldwide information system
8. Regional supranational economic and political communities	8. Worldwide appeal of products
	9. Senior management's long-term commitment to geocentrism as related to survival and growth

And he lists seventeen others that are obstacles in the way of development of the geocentric firm (again eight external and nine internal):

External	Internal
1. Economic nationalism in host and home countries	1. Management inexperience in overseas markets
2. Political nationalism in host and home countries	2. Nation-centred reward and punishment structure

119

External	Internal
3. Military secrecy associated with research in home country	3. Mutual distrust between home country people and foreign executives
4. Distrust of big international firms by host country political leaders	4. Resistance to letting foreigners into the power structure
5. Lack of international monetary system	5. Anticipated costs and risks of geocentrism
6. Growing differences between the rich and poor countries	6. Nationalistic tendencies in staff
7. Host country belief that home countries get disproportionate benefits of international firms' profits	7. Increasing immobility of staff
8. Home country political leaders' attempts to control firm's policy	8. Linguistic problems and different cultural backgrounds
	9. Centralization tendencies in headquarters

Three Prime Tasks

The overcoming of the obstacles is basically a task of attitudinal change. As steps in the building of a new kind of corporate institution, Perlmutter lists a number of fairly simple moves that might be included in a corporation's plan: spreading the ownership of the company worldwide so that the nationals of no single country hold a majority of the equity; having nationals of many countries on the board of directors so that nationals of no single country hold a majority vote; and internationalizing the top management of company so that the enterprise can operate in a nationalistically neutral manner. 'For the main justification of the multinational firm to host and home states will thus be its objective and neutral capacity to facilitate access to the resources of the Global Industrial Estate.' (Global Industrial Estate is Perlmutter's phrase for the unifying world marketplace.)

Secondly, Perlmutter posits the need to plan and implement a worldwide strategy to reach and service markets around the world, which requires facing and overcoming the internal obstacles noted above. Perlmutter suspects that in most companies in most industries this will mean a temporary intermixing of ethnocentric, polycentric, and geocentric approaches, which will represent a tradeoff between aspirations and current restraining forces. In effect the firm will attempt to reduce the costs of ethnocentrism and polycentrism, but not eliminate them entirely in one sudden paroxysm. The key factor here will be the improvement of the climate of trust between persons of differing cultural and national backgrounds.

Perlmutter's third primary task is to develop men for the key positions regardless of their nationality. These men must have first-hand knowledge of and experience in a variety of countries. They must be linguistically fluent. They must also have the traditional management skills – the ability to make decisions, to lead, to evaluate, to communicate, to motivate, to win people's confidence, to listen – but must be able to exercise these capacities with men of widely different backgrounds in crossnational settings.

And finally they must develop syncretic attitudes and values accepting men and ideas for what they are and how they can best be integrated into the corporation's total operations and plans. They must be men capable of defining and carrying through a worldwide mission for their firm.

In more detailed form, Perlmutter summarizes six policies that today's corporations can follow to become truly international and therefore survive in tomorrow's world market.

(1) Improve the capacity to work with host and home political leaders of the right, centre and left, as well as with the more permanent civil servants, with a view to defining how a partnership course can be achieved between the particular international firm and each nation state. The best men are needed for this task.

(2) Develop the capacity to acquire and effectively integrate smaller and medium-sized companies in countries other than one's home base, and to energize them to function effectively as productive parts of a worldwide enterprise. Too frequently the fusion of national interests has proved unproductive, because of distrust between the acquiring group and the acquired. Good people have frequently left and the advantage of the acquisition seemed to be lost.

(3) Create the capacity to develop men for international service. The firms of 1985 will design challenging international careers, both attractive and humanly possible, given the problems of moving men and their families at different stages in life. The problems of re-entry to a home country are serious problems for those who accept international assignments. Only too often, they

121

are forgotten at headquarters, with consequent loss of effectiveness of executives overseas. An obligation of the international firm is to design careers so that the president and managing directors of the future are experienced overseas, and have deep first-hand knowledge of the different regions of the world. The very strategic decisions international corporations must make before 1985 must be based on experience on the spot rather than on hearsay or visits. International careers must recruit the best men from everywhere in the world, not just the best men from the home country. Such a policy requires a systematic programme at the local and head-quarters levels. The man, not his passport, should be the basis of promotion. A further feature of an international career will be that professionals in such a function will feel that they are not only country experts but also meet worldwide standards of excellence. This is one guarantee of getting higher-quality recruits.

(4) Improve the capacity to commit to worldwide objectives personnel at headquarters, at the regional level, and in the subsidiaries, with either product or functional responsibilities. For this, an internationalization process is required at all levels. Some kind of organizational and management development institution is needed in the firms who will survive – to develop executives inside the company, from all over the world. The experience of working together, of knowing other persons from different countries, makes a positive contribution not only to effectiveness at work but also to the creation of the international spirit. This will be a strength of the future international company, as it already is with Philips, Nestle, Unilever, IBM, Royal Dutch/Shell, and many others. The international firm of the future will need to organize for the maintenance of this spirit as it becomes larger and larger, and as more product divisions are formed. Internal organizational and external management development institutions are instruments to achieve these ends.

(5) Increase the capacity to stay in direct contact with the users of company products and services everywhere in the world, and thus to know in which way each user's needs are distinctive, or similar, in each market. This means organizing to build up the necessary market knowledge and skills for the benefit of the user, wherever he is in the world. The worldwide firm must live up to a promise that each customer, in every country, will get not just the

best in the country for his money, but the fruits of knowledge and experience gathered everywhere in the world.

(6) Build trust and confidence among managers and experts of different nations, inside the firm. The key ingredient in building tomorrow's firms is trust and mutual confidence among men of different nations, and acceptance of the distinctive contributions they can make to a worldwide firm. This may not be easy for this generation of industrial leaders in Japan, Europe, and the US. But for the next generation it will be indispensable. I believe that executives can learn how to build confidence and trust by profiting from their errors, rather than explaining them away with such stereotypes as 'you can't work with Brazilians', or French, or Italians, and so forth.

CHAPTER 8

Ansoff and Corporate Strategy

The critical need for rational and methodical determination of corporate strategy is presented by Professor H. Igor Ansoff in more scholarly terms than Perlmutter's need for corporate geocentricity, but Ansoff believes acceptance of his views by top managers is just as consequential for the survival of the firms as does Perlmutter.

Ansoff warns the manager:

Unless [strategic decisions] are actively pursued, they may remain hidden behind the [current] operations problems. Firms are generally slow in recognizing conditions under which concern with the operating problem must give way to concern with the strategic. . . . The immediate demands on management time and effort raised by such operating problems can readily obscure the fact that the basic ills lie not in the firm but in its environment. . . . Since strategic problems are harder to pinpoint, they require special attention. *Unless specific provisions are made for concern with strategy, the firm may misplace its effort in pursuit of operating efficiency at times when attention to strategic opportunities (or threats) can produce a more radical and immediate improvement in the firm's performance.*[1]

At another point,

Exclusive concern with proximate profitability would be almost certain to leave the firm run down at the end of the period. Total emphasis would be on current products and markets . . . *but to remain profitable in the long term, the firm must continue to renew itself*; new resources must be brought in and new products and markets must be developed. Many key phases of this self-renewal

[1] H. Igor Ansoff, *Corporate Strategy.*

activity have long lead times. Therefore, during the proximate period resource commitments must be made to such long-term needs as research and development, management training, and new plants and equipment. If the behaviour of the firm were guided solely by the proximate objective, expenditures for such purposes could not be justified and would be given low priorities. *It is essential, therefore, to establish long-term objectives aimed at maintaining and increasing profitability after the proximate period.*

And finally:

For firms that have no provisions for response to strategic challenges and that refuse to anticipate it, the awareness of the problem usually comes through a traumatic experience . . . the challenge often comes at a time when the firm is ill-prepared to cope with it. . . . Many firms can no longer treat strategic change as a one-time response, put the product-market posture in order, and then revert to operative and administrative concerns. . . .

In the present business environment, no firm can consider itself immune to threats of product obsolescence and saturation of demand. In some industries, surveillance of the environment for strategic threats and opportunities needs to be a continuous process. As a minimum, firms in all industries need to make regular periodic reviews of product-market strategy.

Ansoff's thesis in brief is that those firms that fail to evolve and re-evolve corporate objectives and strategies to attain them will at best be pursuing 'uncoordinated, inefficient, and potentially costly management practices'.

To help firms avoid the possibility that future environmental changes will engulf an unprepared firm, Ansoff has created what amounts to a strategic planning method, based on the method evolved by the US military in the last two decades to determine what would be the best choices to make to maintain an effective establishment at the lowest cost.

In brief, the method consists of six parts:

(1) Perception of decision-needs and/or opportunities plus formulation of alternative courses of action.

(2) Allocation of the firm's resources between opportunities in hand and probable future opportunities, even though there is

insufficient hard and fast knowledge to determine probable profitability and cash flow.

(3) Evaluation of the synergistic effects resulting from the
addition of new products and the penetration of new markets.

(4) Determination of specific opportunities with outstanding
competitive advantages.

(5) Elimination of potential antagonistic objectives between
the existing product-market mix and the new ones.

(6) Evaluation in some detail of specific, individual opportunities despite the lack of hard and fast profitability and cash
flow data.

In sum, this method gives the firm the capability of establishing
a strategy, which is a set of rules for decision making under what
Ansoff calls partial ignorance, i.e. the inability to use simple capital
investment analysis because of the lack of hard and fast market,
cost, and similar data. The working out of the method in essence
calls for the determination of the firm's objectives, self-analysis of
the strong and weak points of the firm, a search of external possibilities for expansion, analysis of these and a determination of how
they fit with the firm's existing objectives and strengths and weaknesses, and finally the determination of the specific opportunities
for expansion and a similar analysis of specific strengths and
weaknesses.

The complexity of the process basically stems from the fact that
the method calls for constant feedback. That is, as each step takes
place, each set of conclusions may affect those drawn from the
previous step which may or may not require altering earlier
conclusions.

Here are descriptions of various elements of the process in
greater detail.

The first and fundamental task in determining a firm's strategy
involves the establishment of the firm's objectives, defined as
'decision rules enabling management to guide and measure the
firm's performance toward its purpose'. Because of the critical
nature of objectives and objective-setting, Ansoff devotes a substantial proportion of his analysis to the definition of objectives
and to considerations as to how a given firm's objectives are
determined and altered.

A company's objectives are often in conflict with each other. Environmental conditions (c.g. new laws, new social attitudes, changes within industries, maturation of technology and technological changes, more or less product-market competition) may change with time, possibly forcing alterations of objectives. Furthermore, the search for and evaluation of new product-markets will indicate that former objectives may have to be modified. While a firm may have a 'goal-threshold' minimum or range, and would reject opportunities for growth that failed to meet the threshold, the threshold goals themselves may change over time.

In other words, objectives themselves change over time. One of the key factors altering them is the strategic method itself – through the process of feedback from the firm's searching and evaluating activities. Obviously a firm will have to lower its objectives if it can find no new projects with which to renew itself that meet its own minimum objective thresholds.

Ansoff presents a systematic set of premises on which the objectives of any firm should be based:

(1) The firm has both economic objectives aimed at optimizing the efficiency of its basic activity – converting its resources into goods and/or services and selling them to customers – and social (i.e. noneconomic) objectives, which are the result of the interaction among individual objectives of the firm's participants.

(2) In most firms the economic objectives exert the primary influence and form the main body of explicit goals used by management to guide and control the firm.

(3) The central purpose of the firm is to maximize long-term return on resources (Ansoff favours optimization of the long-term rate of return on the equity employed in the firm, i.e. profitability, rather than various other 'fancier' measures, e.g. the difference between net present value of revenues and present value of investment).

(4) The social objectives exert a secondary modifying and constraining influence on management behaviour.

(5) In addition to proper objectives two related types of influences are exerted on management behaviour: responsibilities (obligations a firm undertakes to discharge) and constraints (rules excluding certain options from the firm's freedom of action). Neither

127

responsibilities nor constraints necessarily form a part of the firm's internal guidance and control mechanism.

Ansoff very definitely recognizes that many firms are managed in such a way as to maximize profitability in the short term for one reason or another, but such action is obviously not consonant with the central purpose of his own objective, providing a system for corporate continuance and growth over the long term.

While Ansoff notes the growing importance of the concept of the corporation as a social institution and Drucker's concept that the central purpose of the corporation is survival, which in turn requires the placing of less weight on profitability maximization, Ansoff's theory rests on the conservative side of contemporary business thinking.

Of course, the problem with emphasis on profitability as the central corporate objective is the increasing difficulty of measuring it in future years. The further out in time, the more difficult it becomes to use profitability measurement as a criterion, much less as the central one, in the strategy-creation process. Yet he joins Drucker in his emphasis on the need of corporate management to prepare for 'all possible and a good many impossible contingencies'.

Ansoff, therefore, suggests abandonment of efforts to measure long-term profitability. Instead, corporate management must rely on measuring the factors that contribute to long-term profitability. These factors are divided into two broad areas, one involving competitive capabilities, the other corporate flexibility to move in new directions.

Among the competitive measurements are:

(1)   Continuing sales growth at least at the pace of competitors, i.e. no loss of market share;

(2)   Increase in market share to increase relative efficiency;

(3)   Growth in earnings to provide resources for reinvestment;

(4)   Growth in earnings per share to attract new capital;

(5)   Continuing addition of new products and product lines;

(6)   Continuing expansion of the firm's customer population;

(7)   Absence of excessive seasonal or cyclical fluctuations in sales and earnings;

(8)   Turnover ratios (sales divided by working capital, net

worth, inventory, etc.) comparable or better than those of competitors;

(9) Depth of critical skills, of management and skilled personnel;

(10) Yardsticks such as age of plant, machinery, inventory.

Each of these (and other) measurements can be used to set individual objectives, to manage the company, and, most important, to set threshold goals – perhaps threshold yardsticks would be a better term – against which to evaluate new product-market projects.

Because many risks cannot be anticipated or predicted, the firm can be prepared to deal with them only if it has the flexibility to respond. Maintaining flexibility for future catastrophe is something like buying insurance.

There are various ways to achieve corporate flexibility. External flexibility is achieved through a diversified pattern of product-market activities; internal flexibility through liquidity of resources.

External flexibility is in turn divisible into two types, defensive and aggressive. Defensive flexibility minimizes the effect of catastrophe and may be measured:

(1) By the number of different types of customers purchasing substantial portions of the firm's production;

(2) By the number of market segments a firm serves, e.g. a company operating in the US, Europe, and Japan is more flexible than one operating in only one country;

(3) By the number of independent technologies underlying the firm's product-market posture.

Aggressive external flexibility involves the capability of the firm to benefit from future technological breakthroughs. While harder to measure than defensive external flexibility, one measure is the firm's participation in areas of technological ferment (today such areas might be molecular optics or oceanography). Another measure is the relative strength of the firm's research and development in such areas. It is comparatively easy for a company to participate in some other firm's technological breakthrough if it already has an organization to exploit the breakthrough.

Internal flexibility has rather old-fashioned measures: the liquidity of the current ratio, debt to equity ratios, fixed to current asset ratios, etc.

While Ansoff emphasizes profitability or profitability substitutes as central objectives, he does not completely avoid the noneconomic objectives, although he suggests these are constraints (i.e. limits within which a firm operates) rather than objectives (i.e. goals that the firm tries to attain). Among such constraints are philanthropic responsibility, legal constraints such as antitrust laws, job security for employees of the firm, conservative attitude toward risk, maintenance of a favourable corporate image, pursuing policies sought by employees, and a host of other policies.

Analysing types of objectives and even pointing to return on investment as the central one does not solve the critical problem – the determination of just which objectives receive which priority, just how conflicts in objectives are solved.

Ansoff states that three major economic variables affect priorities:

(1) The firm's current and past performance,

(2) The total resources available to the firm, and

(3) The characteristics and opportunities in the external competitive environment. And he emphasizes that pursuance of any one objective (e.g. profitability) at the expense of others (e.g. flexibility) indicates the need for reallocation of priorities.

In other words, the priorities of objectives are not fixed. They are ever changing. Companies at different stages of development will likely have different objective priorities. A highly profitable firm may sacrifice profits for flexibility. A near-monopolistic firm may place reputation at the top of its list, at least for a time.

Ansoff's key point, however, is that 'realistic objectives cannot be arbitrarily decreed in a smoke-filled boardroom. They must be developed through a continuing interaction of objectives and other elements of the strategic problem'. In other words a company's objectives are themselves the functions of the changing business environment, of the external real world in which the firm must deal (as well as the interaction of internal resource availability, management attitudes, etc.).

The method for determination of objectives and their priorities starts with *a priori* choice of basic philosophy, and an explicit statement of the firm's current objectives and priorities. In parallel, an external appraisal of the firm is conducted. The current objectives are evaluated in the light of the appraisal and adjusted accordingly.

If diversification is one of the objectives, for example, then an external appraisal of available opportunities is made. Upon selection of a particular diversification strategy, there is another review of objectives and establishment of a definitive set of objectives – at least for a while when the whole process repeats itself.

Determination as to whether diversification is to become part of a firm's strategy and in what form (various types of acquisitions, mergers, joint ventures with other firms, through research and development, through expansion of existing products and services to more markets, etc.), is the result of the second major part of the strategy process – the internal audit and the external audit.

The internal audit is an analysis of the firm's present skills and resources, its strengths and weaknesses, versus its objectives and aspirations. Ansoff suggests that internal audit be divided into four parts: an audit of operations, of marketing, of general management and finance, and of research and development. Each of these is analysed as to its facilities, its personnel capabilities, its organizational capability, and its management capability.

The internal audit will obviously show different strengths and different weaknesses for different types of firms. A merchandising firm is likely to be weak in research and development, but very strong in consumer marketing know-how.

A capital goods producer knows little about selling mass-market consumer goods, but should be strong in productive capability.

Alongside the internal audit comes the external audit – an analysis of strengths and weaknesses of competitors plus of broad categories of other industries. The analysis of other industries into which the firm might enter will include resources that such entry will require. Perhaps a given firm already has the know-how and capabilities within itself. (For example, a foodstuffs company might already have all the necessary resources to add a new foodstuff product to its line or even a nonfood item that is sold through the same marketing channels and promoted in the same manner as foodstuffs.) On the other hand, the external analysis of a given industry may indicate that the firm has none of the strengths needed to enter it without tremendous additional investment.

The process of external audit (and internal as well) requires the use of synergy analysis, to which Ansoff also devotes considerable thought. Synergy is defined best by the old business adage that a given action should not be planned unless 2 plus 2 equals 5. As a simple example, a merchandising firm obviously has a well-developed marketing network. It faces great difficulty in securing regular supplies of a given product. Therefore it decides to produce the product itself. It gains synergy because it already has the marketing network.

Synergy may be of four different types (or combinations of them). There may be sales synergy. For example, expansion or diversification into a new product may mean use of an already existing distribution network, of already existing promotion and sales administration know-how, or it may mean that the new product complements existing lines or is more profitable because the firm will maximize gains based on its reputation.

Secondly, there may be operating synergy, e.g. the new product, service, or activity may mean higher (or better) utilization of existing facilities, the spreading of overhead over more income items, or it may permit savings from large lot purchasing, or it may reduce the time and money spent on a host of other operating areas.

Thirdly, there is investment synergy, e.g. the possibility of using existing plant and machinery for new products, savings through common inventory controls, or reduced research and development costs because of knowledge 'carry-over'.

And finally, there may be management synergy, perhaps the most important of all and the most difficult to measure in profit and loss terms because of the difficulty of measuring the true cost of the most precious commodity of all, management. There may be management synergy as a result of the reduction in management learning time for a new product or because a certain new product will have a far shorter learning time for the firm's management. In addition, management synergy may result where the new product or market means that there will be no pressures for sharp changes in the firm's existing strategic, organizational, and operating organization, or adds few new problems to the firm.

Obviously, the external appraisal process seeks to find industries – and successively sectors within industries and specific products within sectors – where the synergistic effect is the most positive. Where a given new industry, sector, or product may mean negative synergy, i.e. 2 plus 2 equals less than 4 and no way can be found to alter this situation, the firm rejects it as an item for diversification. Where the synergistic effects are maximized (say they occur to a major extent in all four of the areas noted above) then there is a tentative decision to move into that industry, sector, or product.

In effect, synergy is simply another way of saying that some opportunities for a firm will yield a far higher return on investment than other opportunities. The advantage of the synergy concept is that it provides a specific analytical tool with which to measure strategic choices under 'partial ignorance'. It permits management to estimate profitability of a given future pathway without knowing enough to draw up a pro forma profit and loss statement.

In essence, this is the Ansoff process for strategy formation in full: from objectives to internal appraisal and external appraisal to analysis through various synergy tools, with each successive analysis feeding back through a process of 'successive convergence' until a single, well-ordered, and consistent strategic path is determined, until decisions are made as to which products the firm is to add to (or indeed subtract from) its existing product lines and which markets it is to enter (or indeed withdraw from).

To exemplify a simple strategic pattern, Ansoff uses the example of a chemical company. Its components of strategy are as follows:

(1) *Objectives*: a return on investment of at least 10 per cent (threshold) and a goal of 15 per cent; plus a sales growth goal of 10 per cent a year (threshold 5 per cent a year).

(2) *Strategy*: (a) Product-market scope: basic chemicals and pharmaceuticals. (b) Growth vector: product development and concentric diversification. (c) Competitive advantage: patent protection, superior research competence. (d) Synergy: use of the firm's research capabilities and product technology.

Another firm may find that it must have a strategy based on totally different premises, e.g. it must acquire new products or personnel or know-how or even cash resources. Or it must merge or become a conglomerate to survive.

The key point goes back to the book that Ansoff cites many times, Sloan's book on his years as chairman of General Motors.[1] Sloan emphasizes and re-emphasizes that the secret of his success was his constant battle to get management to devote time to strategic analysis of the future as well as to the ever-pressing and immediate operating problems. In today's world of rapid change, the need for a strategy for the firm despite the lack of knowledge of the details of tomorrow's environment is greater than ever.

[1] *My Years with General Motors.*

133

CHAPTER 9

Amstutz and M.I.S. for Marketing

Professor Arnold Amstutz, who has specialized in corporate utilization of computerized marketing information systems, implicitly shares Perlmutter's and Ansoff's apocalyptic vision: he suggests that a firm that fails to use computers for improved information gathering, storage, analysis, etc., and therefore more effective planning and decision-making, will not survive tomorrow's competitive battle for world markets. In more explicit terms, he states that the computerized system must be carefully focused and controlled by management, not by computer experts. Therefore the firm's top managers must deeply involve themselves in the lengthy process of designing their company's computerized systems – or they run the risk of establishing a system of less than high efficacy, one that fails to meet the firm's (and its managers') needs, or even one that can actually do the firm harm.

The first task of a firm that wishes to develop an effective computerized information system for its marketing operations is to figure out in explicit quantitative terms just how the company makes decisions, how its customers make decisions, and how the elements involved in these two processes interact. This task is not an easy one. It will require, according to Amstutz, the creation of a Task Force of six to eight top executives who have the authority to make corporate policy decisions. And the Task Force will probably have to meet 50–80 hours intermittently over the course of six to eight months (Amstutz estimates), but much more time may be spent.

Perhaps the most crucial thing the Task Force must do is to develop a conceptual framework adapted to the needs of the firm, the information requirements of the industries in which it operates in varying degrees of commitment to measurement and quantitative evaluation, etc. Each participant must examine his own perceptions, objectives, priorities, and performance criteria during the meeting. The conceptual framework of the computerized system that is to eventuate must mirror what top management of the firm wants, with the implicit qualitative criteria converted into explicit quantitative terms.

This is one of the reasons that a company cannot simply hire a group of computer experts and have them set up a system. Outsiders, even if they interview top managers for many hours, cannot possibly figure out just what data should be recorded and made readily available in various forms through the system. Only company management can, and can do so in such a way that the resulting computerized system will be really useful to top management, i.e. will have relevance and improve – and reduce the time of – decision-making. The system must interact with the managers it is to assist; the managers must interact with the assisting system.

The other reason that top management must make up the task force is that top management will understand what it is getting from the computer and why it is getting what it is getting only if it actively figures out how the company and its markets work and only if it transfers all this information to computer programmers. Stated another way, management must itself determine how the computer programme is to be structured or it will not believe the calculations and reports that the computer will spew out.

The Task Force begins to construct decision flow-charts, starting with very broad ones. For example, it may relate the producer to its distributor to its customer. It may relate the company to its competitor, and the sales forces of each company to distributing channels to retailers to customers. Each element in the company's 'action environment' is identified and interrelated by lines showing the interactions of product and information flows.

Having established a limited number of elements and interactions, the Task Force then begins to add complexity. It focuses on the processes that occur at each interaction point and within each element. A product flow-chart would be created. Again, this may be done at first with great simplicity but later taking each sub-element and breaking the processes embodied in them into smaller units.

For example, a product flow-chart would start with raw material records, go to raw material inventory, to raw input, to process delays and goods in process data, to output rate, to finished goods inventory and spoilage rate, to shipping rate. Shipping rate would be followed by transportation delay rates to distributors and finished goods in transit data. The goods would now be moving into the distributor's hands, and the flow-chart continues with distributor finished goods records, distributor finished goods inventory, distributor spoilage rate, and distributor shipping rate, again followed by transportation delay and finished goods in transit (between distributor and retailer) data. Each of the elements of the distributor sector would be repeated for the retailer sector. Each of these records can be measurable in dollar terms.

For an industrial goods firm, similar data flows might be maintained by the producer for the customer. A consumer goods company, on the other hand, might well develop a flow-chart describing consumer exposure and reaction to advertising or other forms of promotion.

After the Task Force completes the detailing of the flow-charts representing interaction points of each element in the company's action environment, it proceeds to identify major decision points associated with each element, i.e. those points inside and outside the company where decisions are made that would vary the sales and profits of the firm.

The next step is to determine what factors influence specific decisions and responses. At this point it is necessary to convert management's intuitive understanding of market processes to explicit and testable behaviour models. Relationships between decision inputs and observable behaviour are formulated in terms permitting validation against available market data. Dozens of criteria might be established. For example, in marketing: consumers under age 20 do not buy TV sets. Consumers who buy homes, buy one TV set within sixty days of purchase of the home in four out of five cases, say. Consumers in high income brackets buy a colour TV set with a large screen in so many cases under certain circumstances. The price of a TV set plays a major part in increasing sales of different models. Such and such a percentage of TV sets are sold through discount stores. Any number of verifiable factors might be identified and perhaps interrelated with each other. The Task Force may decide that some of the formulas are not sufficiently consequential to include in its system.

After the early stages of the Task Force work, it is joined by one or all the members of a Project Group, whose task it is to implement the relevant planning parameters, flow-charts, and decision factors developed by the Task Force. (The Project Group is made up of operating managers, including those who will operate the computer itself.) The Project Group also operates alone testing and refining elements, interaction points, decision factors, etc. It may suggest alternative structures to the Task Force that seem more valid. In the end major elements and processes in the 'action environment' are identified, and measures and models describing their interactions specified and validated. The company now can move to the next phase of installing a computerized information system.

The new stage establishes the specific corporate planning and decision procedures to be supported by the system; the factors in the environment to be monitored; the models and measures to be used and the functions to be performed; and establishment of criteria for evaluating system performance. The project group then determines the specific computers and programmes and procedures to be used, and arranges for installation of the equipment and systems. The final phase involves implementation with in-house equipment and trained personnel, familiarization of management with the specifics of using the system, and final determination of procedures for reviewing and modifying it as experience with it takes place.

WHAT THE COMPUTER CAN DO

Amstutz has developed a comparatively simple manner to describe the capabilities of a computerized marketing information system. He divides the capabilities into five broad dimensions or characteristics, each of which is analysable into subdimensions.

The first of the five dimensions Amstutz calls MANAGEMENT ACCESS (MA). MA is defined as the time it takes for a manager to get data from the system, i.e. how many minutes, hours, days, or months does it take for a manager to have a question answered.

A company will no doubt have a system where MA for certain types of data may be a good deal longer than for others. Some types of data will be programmed to spew out very rapidly; others, where unusual conglomerations of raw data in the system must be surveyed, will take much longer.

Or the company may divide up access time by departments so that MA for the same question may vary in accordance with the time the question is asked. If Department A can ask the computer questions only in the morning, but manager x of Department A asks the question in the afternoon, he must wait until the following morning. Or a firm may rent time at a service bureau and have access to it only one day a week. The development of multiuser computers is eliminating much of this type of delay.

The biggest MA factor is whether the manager seeking data has direct access to the system or relays his questions through specialized staff. Some systems are designed 'on-line' in which the manager has his own input and output consoles, with which he can ask for data and receive a response. While on-line systems are used by some companies, Amstutz warns that on-line systems can lead to troubles, mainly because of the ambiguity danger where the computer does not understand what the manager may want, provide something other than that sought, and, after a few similar cases, convince the manager not to use his on-line facility or trust the computer. Amstutz predicts that on-line systems will continue to be rare.

Rather, the manager will ask specialized employees for data, employees who are thoroughly intimate with computer language and other intricacies. Use of specialized employees obviously lengthens MA time.

In an analysis of a wide range of computerized information systems used by large US companies, MA time was designed to be from twenty-four hours to five days in the case of about half the firms. Only about 10 per cent had access time of one minute or less (i.e. on-time). The bulk of the remaining companies had access times of one to eight hours.

The second dimension Amstutz calls INFORMATION RECENCY (IR), which is defined as the time lapse between the occurrence of an event and the inclusion of the data describing the event in the computerized system. Stated another way, IR is the time required to incorporate data in the system (versus MA, which is the time it takes a manager to get data already included in the system).

Here again the firm has choices as to how fast it wants the system to operate. It can decide, for example, that data on each sale will be entered into the system every month, every week, or every hour. Indeed, it could even structure the system so that each sale is entered into the system a few moments after it occurs. The latter is called 'real time', the entering of transactions or events into the system as they occur. Of course, IR can be different for different events and data; it may be that certain transactions are entered into the system every day, while other transactions are entered every week or month.

As with on-line MA, Amstutz throws cold water on the effervescence of computer salesmen pushing real time IR, at least as regards marketing data. Amstutz suggests that real time IR can be dangerous, since it can cause management to give undue attention to recent events while ignoring more significant longer-term trends.

Of major US companies, only about one in twenty use real time IR. About a third of the firms entered data one to twenty-four hours after time of occurrence. About another third entered data two to four weeks after occurrence.

The third dimension Amstutz calls INFORMATION AGGREGATION (IA), defined as the detail at which information is maintained in the system. For example, the lowest level of data aggregation would be to have each individual transaction entered into and available for retrieval from the system. On the other hand, data may be aggregated at entry, and at output into various aggregation levels. For example, data on total sales, sales by region, by each salesman, etc.

A given company, as with IR, may have different IA factors for different events or different types of information. For example, an inventory control system would have to use a very low level of aggregation, or it would be useless. The system would have to show the number of product components of each type (and preferably with very recent IR) to fulfil its function. On the other hand, market share statistics that, say, come in monthly, are by nature highly aggregated figures.

Amstutz is a proponent of disaggregation, i.e. entering marketing data on a sale-by-sale basis and having a flexible capability of aggregating each sale in any way one might want later to use. (Amstutz calls the lowest level of aggregation line-item aggregation, which is really no aggregation at all.)

In the study of actual US corporate practice, about half of all firms use the line items as the lowest level of data aggregation, another 5 per cent each invoice, another 14 per cent the brand, and 24 per cent the product. Among companies planning new computer systems, these figures are 55 per cent, 23 per cent, 5 per cent, and 14 per cent, indicating that disaggregate entries are becoming much more common.

139

The fourth dimension, ANALYTIC SOPHISTICATION, describes just how complex a set of operations the computer can carry out. Amstutz indicates eight basic levels of increasing sophistication of operations:

(1) The computer merely retrieves data in the system.

(2) The computer adds various figures together in the system.

(3) The computer averages and finds differences of various figures in the system.

(4) The computer classifies and aggregates data in various ways.

(5) The computer extrapolates from historical data, analyses variances, and makes forecasts (assuming no changes in the basic assumptions).

(6) The computer relates the various elements, decision factors, and interactions noted earlier in the chapter and permits managers to relate each element in the flow patterns to each other. Managers can use the computer to see how the overall process of the company's operations and 'action environment' are changing over time, and can be alerted to figure out changes in corporate policies in response.

(7) The computer breaks down the elements, decision factors, and interactions into their smallest pieces and permits managers to test out the effect of different corporate actions. With this level of sophistication, the manager can, for example, see what is likely to happen to sales if advertising expenditures are doubled or concentrated on different media. Or what would happen if any of hundreds of other possible changes in the company's policies and strategies were to be made.

(8) The computer can itself alter the assumptions concerning the 'action environment' that have been programmed into it, as sales and other data are entered into the system indicating that the original assumptions were changing. The computer monitors the environment, notes changing relationships, and changes these relationships in its own programme.

The last three levels of sophistication are called macro-process models, micro-analytic behavioural models, and adaptive heuristics by those initiated into the language of the computer expert.

Almost all us firms using computerized marketing information systems utilize the first five levels of computer sophistication, but relatively few (about a third) utilize macro-process models (level six) and micro-analytic simulation (level seven). Very few indeed use adaptive heuristics.

One of the reasons for the relatively small portion of companies using the more advanced levels of sophistication is the relatively small number of companies that have gone through the Task Force–Project Group operation, noted earlier in the chapter, and therefore the small number of firms whose management would have confidence in the computer 'telling the truth' in these areas.

There is a tendency of firms that have had increasing experience with a computerized marketing information system to move into the more sophisticated levels, probably because management has accumulated more confidence in the computer's mathematics and analysis as it has had more experience with it.

The real advantage of those companies whose management 'understands' the computer lies in Amstutz's fifth and final dimension, SYSTEM AUTHORITY, meaning how much management delegates to the computer. Amstutz defines seven levels of greater and greater delegation of authority:

(1) Simple retrieval of data.

(2) Check of data to insure against gross clerical error.

(3) Monitoring events, e.g. noting when various programmed check points are reached.

(4) Recommending action, e.g. suggesting which is the appropriate response to a given nontypical occurrence discovered through monitoring.

(5) Acting, actually carrying out the action recommendation, e.g. writing a letter to a past due customer, placing an order.

(6) Predicting future developments, sales, costs, etc. This may be done on the basis of no change in assumptions (analogous to sophistication level five) or with changing assumptions (analogous to sophistication levels six and seven).

(7) Learning, which is analogous to the eighth level of analytic sophistication (adaptive heuristics).

There are few problems in delegating the first four levels just noted: retrieving, detecting gross clerical errors, monitoring, and recommending. And most firms do delegate these functions to the computer.

Many companies have the computer analyse data in various ways. Examples include sales statistics, detailed in an almost infinite number of different ways (by geographic area, by specific customers, by salesman, over various time periods with comparisons to past performance over various time periods); market activity reports such as market shares, competitor activity, changing trends in the external environment, statistically significant adverse or favourable sales trends, and even estimates of likelihood of a new product's success in a given area; and information on internal operating processes and performance measures.

But managers in most firms are loath to have the computer actually carry out corporate actions. Amstutz's study showed only 8 per cent of US firms delegating the power to act on its own to the computerized information system.

And while a very much larger percentage of firms draw forecasts of various sophistication levels from the system, there is often strong disbelief in or hostility to computerized forecasts among managers.

Where the computerized system has been installed without the Amstutz Task Force–Project Group operation, the manager will probably begin to accept computerized forecasts only after he has had an opportunity to test these forecasts against actual developments over time. Often, just as the manager begins to accept the computer's predictions, they cease being very accurate because the assumptions programmed into the forecasting model begin to change.

Amstutz feels that this situation strongly supports his thesis that the manager must be thoroughly familiar with the computerized system structure, which is best accomplished through being involved in its creation. The manager must understand the models on which system decisions and predictions are based.

Because so many managers do not comprehend what is going on in the computer and therefore mistrust much of its highly potential usefulness to the firm – in the three highest levels of sophistication, it appears quite likely that those firms that do have managers capable of understanding, and therefore controlling, all aspects of computerized marketing information system potential will tend to make wiser actions earlier and gain an increasing share of market from those firms that fail to use the computer to its fullest.

According to Amstutz, if an information system is to support management planning and decision processes, it must incorporate models or data structures that link market response to management action. The problems inherent in such management-oriented model development are great. It is not sufficient for the system designer to establish a precise quantitative structure. To be useful for management system design, the structure must be understood by management and reflect its perceptions of the market environment and the planning and decision process. To achieve such a structure the system analyst must work with management to convert initially vague and ambiguous statements into explicit and objectively verifiable models. Management must understand and accept the conceptual structuring of system requirements to define explicitly the measures and analytic procedures to be encompassed by the system. If this level of communication is not achieved, it may be impossible to develop a system that will be used by management.

CHAPTER 10

Management Development

During the past two decades, management has been recognized as the most important of corporate resources, and as the most crucial of corporate assets. Only capable management can assure maximum utilization of a firm's other resources. Without capable management, capital can be frittered away, advanced technology can be wasted, solid market networks allowed to atrophy. And most serious, without capable managers in sufficient numbers, all sorts of new opportunities must be allowed to fall into competitive hands.

Capable management has been recognized as the key asset because it has come into such short supply in recent years. Availability of capable and experienced managers has not kept up with the rapid growth of corporate sales, or with the rapid geographic spread of the business of most companies, or with the rapid product diversification of many corporations. In the meantime, technology has been advancing, causing management obsolescence: more and more managers are unable to keep pace with the new breakthroughs and the new ways of thinking and acting.

Every forecast of the availability of capable management in the coming decades indicates that the shortage will continue and probably grow worse. The opportunities for corporate growth will continue to multiply, but the number of creative managers being spawned by the world's educational systems will not keep pace. The only solution is for companies themselves to create their own development programmes. And that is exactly what the larger firms in the US have been doing over the past decade or more.

THE ESSENTIAL CAPABILITIES

When management development was first proposed as a management technique, it was criticized on the ground that managers are

144

born, not taught. This criticism has grown muted in recent years. Here are the management capabilities that one large US-based international firm believes are necessary for success and believes can be taught.

(1)   Knowledge of, and experience with: (a) relevant technologies; (b) cause–effect relationships; (c) internal organization and external environment.

(2)   Decisiveness: the capacity to take decisions committing the organization to lines of action even in the fact of uncertainty and risk.

(3)   Responsibility: the capacity to assume obligation and to take the consequences of decision.

(4)   Vision: the capacity to visualize the range of the possible and the probable and to translate these potentials into actuality.

(5)   Initiative: the capacity to act in situations that lack structure and direction – to provide that structure.

(6)   Leadership: the capacity to energize others and to bring them to levels of performance that they, if left to their own devices, would not attain.

(7)   Sensitivity to situations and to people. This leads to the capacity for cooperation and team play.

(8)   Resilience: the capacity to hold one's course in spite of repeated shocks.

(9)   Autonomy: the capacity to 'go it alone', to be self-sufficient, but at the same time, reactive to the demands of others.

On the basis of expected changes in the company's environment over a period of some years, this firm has added two more capabilities. Most significant is the greatly extended range of variables that will have to be taken into consideration by managers as they arrive at decisions, and as they judge conditions, consequences, and results. *The capacity to deal with complexity, to conceptualize totalities, and to translate abstractions into effective action will therefore be mandatory.* This requirement will be of far more importance in the future than it has been in the past.

The capability for synthesis is equally relevant: in a world demanding new forms and approaches, the capacity to put together new combinations, both conceptually and in action, will become more and more strategic.

This firm also believes that there will be particular new challenges as regards development of staff and service units within the company. The necessity to provide liaison and coordinating units to fill gaps between operating units will increase. With the advent of computers and new communication systems, service units must be developed to design, to conceptualize, to service, and to control.

Capabilities must, therefore, be developed in the 'staff' area. Here a fine balance of sensitivity, perceptiveness, and social skill is required. This capability must be developed in depth in organizations.

At operating levels, we can anticipate a heavier emphasis upon *ad hoc* teams set up to deal with specific problems and tasks. The capacity to work in teams or groups of associates will, therefore, be at a premium.

Finally, new roles will develop. One of these, the role of the non-person, a designation coined by Professor Richard Neustedt of Columbia University, will enter the organizational scene. Reference here is to the individual who is not formally a member of the organization, who moves in and out, yet who knows the organization. Not constrained by formalities, he can move with freedom and he can act. In effect, he will serve as external staff.

THE SCIENCE OF MANAGEMENT DEVELOPMENT

The science of management development itself consists of establishment of three types of programmes:

(1) *Selection Processes*: the development of job descriptions and the matching of individuals to fit these descriptions.

(2) *Experience Planning*: the movement of individuals through a series of experiences and jobs so that the requisite experiences are provided.

(3) *Education*: the providing of opportunities for individuals to further their education either through additional formal schooling or through in-company programmes.

The large US-based firm whose case study is being presented here has taken these three components and has created the following more detailed management development plan:

1. Selection

The capabilities we have outlined above provide the criteria for selection. Given the requisite technical competence, candidates should be selected on the basis of these requirements.

The key problem facing us is that of developing indices of these capabilities, indices indicative of potential. Techniques of measurement must then be devised that can be demonstrated to be both reliable and valid.

Assuming for the moment the development of such indices and measures, we face the task of determining the right manpower mix. If we are concerned with the selection of personnel for management in an international corporation, what ratios of domestic and other nationals should there be? Today the policy ideally is to have affiliates staffed by managers and personnel indigenous to the country involved. Corporate personnel and top management, however, tend to be from the home country. Change in this tendency will be required if a truly international character is to evolve.

2. Experience

We start, then, if our selection processes are sound, with individuals who have given evidence of possessing the necessary capabilities. It then becomes necessary to provide them with the necessary experiences to transform potential into actuality.

If we can assume that 'like produces like', it follows that individuals must be placed in positions where they can experience decision, where they must exercise leadership, assume responsibility, and develop their perceptiveness and sensitivity. They must be placed in positions where they enter and assimilate cultures and develop understanding.

This requires effective career planning. Before realistic planning can occur, however, a knowledge of the total complex of positions within an organization must be completed. And this must be done in terms of organizations as they evolve and are transformed by the future.

Each position must be seen, not only in terms of its relationship to the organization, but also in relation to the contribution each can make to the development of individuals.

With knowledge of this kind, planning can be done. Sequences of positions can be structured so that individuals move through

K*

them in a systematic way according to plan and when they are ready. We do not clearly know the limits that should be considered relative to the duration of assignment in any given position or in any given country. Is it better, for example, to alternate assignments for international personnel between the home base and abroad, or should we develop an international career service? Should we develop purely 'staff' career lines or should we alternate individuals between 'line' and 'staff'? Indeed should any distinction be made between 'international' and 'domestic', between 'line' and 'staff'?

3. *Education*

If we think of education as a process of learning that prepares individuals for their station in life, a process continuing throughout their existence, then our considerations centre upon what has been called 'continuing education'.

The kinds of education most necessary before the individual enters his career are still open questions. Whether a 'liberal arts' education, a professional degree, or a mixture is most necessary, we do not know with any certainty.

a. Formal Education. The forms that education can take are many. For the manager of the international company of tomorrow, however, the following appear to be relevant: A firm and thorough grounding in at least one major discipline, whether this be in the physical sciences, the humanities, the social sciences or a professional field; a renewing of this grounding at periodic intervals by refresher courses will be required; a general understanding and appreciation of the knowledge underlying the business of the organization. This would include, in addition to technical areas, an acquaintance with the key functional areas and a thorough grounding in the culture and socio-economic system of the country in which the individual will be assigned. We have stated the need for sensitivity. It may be that this kind of sensitivity is an inherent personality characteristic not capable of being learned. To what extent it is susceptible to training must be studied. An opportunity to develop other fields of knowledge as that individual sees fit must be provided.

Recent developments in 'programmed learning' give us opportunities to shorten learning time. Obviously we should take advantage of this advance and move toward the refinement and extension of this technique. We should also take advantage of Centres for Continuing Education that many universities are developing.

These approaches are, of course, clear even though they probably are not systematically utilized. Needless to say, they should be.

Yet even though the methods are available, the perplexing problem of allocating time for these endeavours confronts us. The time of any manager is taken up with the responsibilities of doing business. Where does he find the time for *education*?

Left to his own devices, he probably will not. It would appear, therefore, that the time must be planned by the organization, that responsibility for education be part of the duties of every manager both with regard to himself and those reporting to him, and that there be a pay-off for the discharge of these responsibilities in terms of salary and promotion.

b. Nonformal Education. Formal education constitutes only a small part of the education of the individual. The everyday process of living and of work 'educates' and makes up the major share.

To the greatest extent possible, then, experience must be provided to the manager so that he becomes the truly educated man. Job rotation is, of course, a partial answer. But we need to search for other avenues, understand better the value of particular experiences, and move accordingly. The task of achieving an education is brilliantly described in the book, *The Education of Henry Adams*, by Henry Adams, Boston. It should be read by every executive.

Any good approach to a given task requires a carefully devised control system. Standards of performance must be articulated, feedback instituted, and intervention processes structured to guarantee the effectiveness of programmes designed to meet environmental demands and operating requirements.

Such control processing must be applied to the development of managers. To sum up: (a) the setting of standards of performance in relationship to the demands of the environment; (b) the institution of workable feedback mechanisms from the individual to the organization and, of equal importance, from programmes to management in terms of their effectiveness; (c) taking corrective action so that we know the right patterns of development are occurring.

Today, programmes in management development all too often exist in a vacuum without relationship to requirements and without adequate control. Obviously this should be corrected.

UNANSWERED QUESTIONS

In the above remarks, following a systematic approach to the problem of management development, we have attempted to indicate a series of key orienting concepts. We have felt it necessary to derive our thinking from considerations of changes in the environment and the resulting organizational responses. Any other approach moves in a vacuum without proper foundation.

Our sketch had to be brief. No doubt many gaps exist and many assumptions will be proven to be incorrect. However, a start has been made. Further developments must await the results of systematic and planned studies at all levels.

In order to guide this necessary inquiry, the following unanswered questions are raised.

(1) Our definition of 'management development' was primarily oriented toward meeting organizational needs. Is this sufficient, or does management have a responsibility beyond this extending to the realization of the full potential of all its personnel?

(2) How do we measure the cost of management development, and what criteria do we follow in allocating scarce resources to this endeavour?

(3) What are the processes of human development as they occur in the adult, in the middle and later years? We must know more about these processes if we are realistically to structure programmes for development throughout the career of the individual.

(4) What are the 'developmental tasks' that must be passed through as the individual moves from one level to another? From one culture to another?

(5) What happens to an individual 'psychologically' when he must move from one culture to another? When he fails?

(6) How can we maintain the personal development of the 'comer' who falls by the wayside as the road becomes more complex and rougher?

(7) How can managers be motivated to develop others when the key pay-offs are in terms of operating performance?

(8) How can we provide individuals with a sense of identity and loyalty in an international company? In another sense, can a

150

company, and its people become truly international in character? More importantly, is it a desirable goal?

(9) How can we provide middle management and staff levels with work that has a meaning in an age of specialization and automation?

(10) Recently, many writers on management development have insisted that development is the individual's responsibility. While to a considerable extent, self-development must occur, is this all that is necessary? What is management's role in insisting upon development and taking the necessary steps to make certain it is accomplished?

(11) The manager of tomorrow must adopt the characteristics of Renaissance Man – a man capable of experiencing a broad range of subjects. What kind of environment and what kinds of experiences are most conducive to developing that kind of personality?

(12) How do we, as managers, provide time for our subordinates to acquire the necessary education and training as they move through their careers?

(13) What indices and measuring sticks do we use in identifying managerial potential in the international fields of the future, and how can we put these to use so that they are effective in the development process?

SOME MANAGEMENT DEVELOPMENT PROBLEMS

Development may vary with a company's organizational structure, but most companies would add that the programme should be centralized at the corporate level. As Ford put it: 'The success of any management development programme is in direct proportion to the freedom with which people can be moved around in the organization.' Nevertheless, formulating the ideal of corporate centralization of management development presents obvious difficulties when the management development department wishes to employ techniques that may effect the immediate interests of a division or department. If the head of a subsidiary or division is treated as having direct responsibility for the profit performance of his unit, there are obvious difficulties in limiting his right to select and retain managerial talent who in the management development department's view, ought to be moved to another department or division. To resolve such conflicts, the management development department must have enough backing from the chief executive or the board of directors.

Where a company is divisionalized, the management development programme can also be divisionalized. Many us companies began formal development programmes in one or more of their domestic divisions long before they established them in their international division. But this practice is worthwhile only if it is part of a long-term programme to spread management development throughout the company. A firm wastes opportunities for developing people and (if division-to-division transfers are limited) arbitrarily favours some of its rising managers in those divisions that do have programmes at the expense of those that do not.

A second organizational problem that must be surmounted is geographical dispersion. Where the development programme covers only one country or one nationality (i.e. that of the parent company), it is obviously easier to create and administer. But such a programme starts out with one hand tied. A large number of potential top managers may be automatically eliminated from consideration and development.

A third problem for the divisionalized company with a large number of foreign affiliates is the difficulty of transferring men from one division to another, particularly of transferring men from the parent company to foreign assignments.

This problem seems to have been resolved by most companies. The first and foremost technique is a clear statement, backed by deeds, from the chief executive officer, of the importance of increasing foreign business to the company as a whole. It may even extend to a statement that future top management must necessarily have foreign line or staff experience as a precondition of promotion to high office.

Secondly, a long-term educational programme may be used to back the president's words with proof. Often, the proof is provided simply by the rising percentage of foreign sales and earnings in the company, along with an educational process including foreign trips for top domestic division management. Another solution to the opposition of domestic management giving up its best people for foreign service is demonstration of the need and the advantages in sales and profits to those who cooperate.

In some companies management development is the responsibility of a special committee. Those that plan management development more systematically appoint a full-time officer, who is often called the Management Development Manager, or (and the connotation is significant) Management Development Advisor.

More important than the name of the functional position is the position of the management development expert in the corporation. He must be close to top corporate management. A good case can be made for the theory that the management development department be supervised not by the vice president in charge of personnel affairs, but rather by the vice president in charge of corporate planning.

Before defining what a management development function involves, it is vital to say what a management development specialist should not be dealing with. Most firms believe that he ought not to be concerned with the recruiting of personnel – except in those cases where companies apply management development to graduates the moment they sign on. As a rule he should be a talent spotter of people who have been with the company for some time. (Some corporations lay down rules that management development is not to start until after five or ten years of employment.)

It is not the management development department's job to appraise people for promotion or salary increases. This negative rule is considered of such significance that most companies ask departmental heads to file, at different periods of the year, two appraisal reports: one dealing with a person's work performance with recommendations of salary increases and promotions, and another dealing with his potential as a senior manager. If only one appraisal report is made, departmental heads may tend to describe a person's management acumen in a more favourable light than it deserves, if this is the only way to attain salary increases for him. There must be a clear division between recommendations for rewards for good work performance and the evaluation that marks out a man as a future senior general manager.

The management development function does involve:

The maintenance of a highly detailed organization chart of all the firm's management positions, high-level nonmanagerial positions, and the likely positions to be created in the foreseeable future.

Knowledge of who fills each of these positions, how long these positions will be filled by the incumbent, who are unlikely candidates to replace them at the appropriate time, and who are candidates for new positions.

A system for identifying all managerial candidates, and finding out whether a given employee wishes to enter managerial positions.

A complete and continually updated index of all possible managerial candidates within the company.

An appraisal system of management candidates that regularly updates the progress of the candidates, with control as to how the appraisals are made.

Some control over the work that the candidates are given.

Where a given candidate fails to reach a given objective, the right to prevent his dismissal, and to provide him with an alternative position.

The power to transfer people who are being groomed for higher positions from one unit to another. This may be through direct control, although this is extremely rare, or through the ability to convince a line officer to let a man go or to take someone on, backed up by the support of the highest management of the company.

Providing counsel and assistance to managerial candidates in relation to the functions of the development department.

Learning about and using internal and external programmes to develop managers.

Few firms have given all these functions to this development officer or committee, but all of them in one form or another are necessary for a fully effective programme.

While the management development department is responsible for developing managers companywide, there is no question that the line officer is responsible for day-to-day development of the managerial candidates under him. Many firms make it clear to each of their managers that they have the task of grooming a successor, and that they can enhance their own upward movement in the management hierarchy by assuring that a replacement is available. But these firms also make it clear that the manager is rated on how well he develops not only a single replacement but all the managerial candidates under his control. A management development programme is not a substitute for line officers who think and act in terms of a company's overall objectives. The objective of both the programme and every good manager is the same by definition.

The Development of Human Resources

BOHDAN HAWRYLYSHYN
Director, Centre d'Études Industrielle, Geneva

I think what is implied in most business discussions, and sometimes made more explicit, is at least one common precondition for successful operation of the firm of the future. And that common precondition is the quality of human resources at its disposal; the will and ability of its people to learn new knowledge and apply it; their capability to make a commitment to some organizational goals; their ability to focus their energy on selected purposes of the firm. The most important element in the human resources of the firm would of course be the managers, because they have multiplying effects. It is the managers that have to use all the resources of the firm in trying to achieve its objectives.

We talk about management education, we talk about management training, we talk about management development and organizational development. These four activities are complementary; their ultimate objective is the same, although they seem almost in opposition to each other. Let me just briefly state what I mean by them.

This process of management education is the activity that is focused on man, and the objective of it is to try to expand the whole range of capabilities of a manager, in this case, so that he could confront a number of tasks – some of them even unforeseeable. So it is this broad, educational process that increases the range of capabilities of the manager.

Management training is the activity that has been more narrowly focused on the job, job oriented rather than man oriented. Here the purpose and objective of training is to prepare man, or a group of people, for accomplishment of specific known tasks within a known job context. That is, we know that we want to utilize a certain procedure, or set of techniques. Let us say that we want in a firm to go to a direct costing system. We collect a group of our accountants, take them through a training scheme on direct costing, and

hope that the Monday after we can immediately shift to the implementation of that particular approach or procedure. To re-state, it
is job oriented, the purpose of it is to prepare man, or groups of
people, to perform specific known tasks in a known job context.

However, management development is an activity that actually
does or should encompass first learning of the job, because the bulk
of learning in management clearly still has to take place on the job.
But management development, if thought out, aims to enhance the
opportunities of learning on the job. We can also intermittently
include some exposures to management training and management
education, hopefully all of that within some sort of a career plan.
So it is a designed activity for a continuous process of growth
development of people through learning on the job, learning on
training programmes, learning on educational programmes.

But so far, all these activities are essentially focused on an
individual. Sometimes we use groups of people but essentially we
aim at improving the capability of a man. In addition to that, and
more recently, a greater preoccupation and greater energy is
focused on organizational development, where we do not just
address ourselves to a man, but try to change the whole organization
by actually working on its units first. So we try to develop teams,
groups, within an organization, that can function more effectively,
and through that process we can actually try to transform the whole
organization so that it will function more effectively.

The first thing that we have to do in our work as managers is to
perceive problems or opportunities. We have to pick up the signals
that something has to be done. Secondly, we have to gather some
data and assign some priorities. In other words we cannot cope
with all the problems and all the opportunities immediately, and at
once. Some of them we may wish to discard immediately because
they are not overly important. Then we have to gather pertinent
information. Once we have that information, we go through the
process of analysing it, to find out what the problems or opportunities really are. We then go through this process of generating or
formulating alternative solutions to problems. We then decide or
choose from available alternatives, and then we have to implement
the decisions through the process of good leadership. That is
communication, motivation, and in order to be able to carry out
that cycle of activities we have to have a certain set of very specific
skills, and to be able to perceive progress, opportunities. We have

to have sensitive perception, capacity to observe, to perceive in a certain way.

Finally, to be able to implement decision, you really have to have these leadership skills, which mean effective communication capability, so that others not only understand you but accept what it is that you are trying to get across, and the capacity to motivate; that is, to get people to do their utmost.

The skills that we have just tried to describe can be developed even in a school setting by simulating certain activities. To develop the skill to perceive you have to get involved in the observation of real life problems. The method that can achieve that, therefore, is some sort of work in the field – consulting projects, for example.

Secondly, to be able to develop this capacity to generate appropriate information there is now a method called Incident Method which simulates this activity of asking relevant questions to get relevant information. To be able to develop diagnostic skill, you have to go through the process of analysing problems over and over again, and the case method is still by far the best one to develop that capability.

In management know-how, we have two rather distinctive components: one, the technology of management – this whole set of quantitative techniques, that allows us to deal with problems, phenomena, things. It allows us to manipulate things. The characteristic of the technology of management is the fact that it is universally valid, it can be transferred, it can be generated.

There is another component of management know-how, however, that has relevance here, which I would call the sociology of management. This is the know-how that allows us to structure and lead effective human organizations. Unlike the technology of management, the sociology of management is not readily transferable.

To be able to manage in different countries, and even more across different national borders, managers have to be aware of national differences. To prepare managers for international operations through educational programmes, one must somehow bring to them at the knowledge level an awareness of environmental differences.

At the attitudinal level we have to be able to help managers to be willing to accept and adapt to these differences. It is one thing to know that they exist, but another thing to say, as we often do here in Europe, 'of course you do it differently in France, but the American way is the best way and we have proved it.'

Finally, at the skill level we have to develop this ability to choose between the things that you must adapt to, and things that you can ignore while you innovate. In Japan, there are a lot of things that you can bring with you, be it from Switzerland or the United States, but some things, like life-long employment, had better be respected, at least for the time being.

Given the fact that firms are internationalizing rapidly, more and more attention has to be paid to this transition from domestic careers to international careers. Experience shows that success domestically does not guarantee success at the international level, or abroad. In fact, we have observed a number of rather dramatic failures of this kind. So there is some sort of special educational mission that has to be carried out to prepare people for this transition, and again a new type of methodology allows us to achieve this fairly effectively. When it comes to firms, clearly the critical element of their human resources is managers. A whole range of activities can help us enhance their quality. It ought to be a continuous process. There are elements of learning on the job that are important. There is some sort of training focusing on the accomplishment of specific tasks that is important. But management education can, and should, play a rather catalytic role in this process.

BIBLIOGRAPHY

AMSTUTZ, ARNOLD E.

Computer Simulation of Competitive Market Response. Cambridge, Mass.; M.I.T. Press, 1967.

ANDREWS, KENNETH RICHMOND

Business Policy; text and cases. With Edmund P. Learned, C. Roland Christensen, and William D. Guth. Homewood, Ill., Irwin, 1965; revised edition, 1969.
The Case Method of Teaching Human Relations and Administration. An interim statement. (Collection of papers.) Cambridge, Mass., Harvard University Press, 1953.
The Effectiveness of University Management Development Programs. With research assistance from Daniel J. McCarthy and others. Boston, Mass., Harvard University, Division of Research, 1966.
Nook Farm; Mark Twain's Hartford circle. Hamden, Conn., Shoe String Press, 1967 (Archon Books); University of Washington Press, 1969.

ANSOFF, H. IGOR

Business Strategy; selected readings. Harmondsworth, Penguin Books, 1969 (Penguin Modern Management Readings. Penguin Education X72.)
Corporate Strategy. An analytic approach to business policy for growth and expansion. New York, McGraw-Hill, 1965; Harmondsworth, Penguin, 1970.

GALBRAITH, JOHN K.

The Affluent Society. London, Hamish Hamilton, 1961.
Ambassador's Journal; a personal account of the Kennedy years. Boston, Mass., Houghton Mifflin, 1969; London, Hamish Hamilton, 1969.
American Capitalism; the concept of countervailing power. Boston, Mass., Houghton Mifflin, 1962; London, Hamish Hamilton, 1957.
Economic Development. Revised and enlarged edition. Boston, Mass., Houghton Mifflin, 1964.
Economic Development in Perspective. Cambridge, Mass., Harvard University Press, 1962.
Economics, Peace and Laughter. Boston, Mass., Houghton Mifflin, 1971.
Economics and the Art of Controversy. Tacoma, Washington, College of Puget Sound, 1954. (Brown and Haley Lectures.)

159

The Great Crash 1929; with a new introduction. Boston, Mass., Houghton Mifflin, 1961; Harmondsworth, Penguin, 1969.
How to Control the Military. New York, Doubleday, 1969; N.C.L.C., 1970
Indian Painting; the scene, themes and legends. Co-authored with Mohindar Singh Randhawa. London, Hamish Hamilton, 1969.
Journey to Poland and Yugoslavia. Cambridge, Mass., Harvard University Press, 1958; London, Oxford University Press, 1959.
The Liberal Hour. Boston, Mass., Houghton Mifflin, 1960; London, Hamish Hamilton, 1960.
Made to Last. London, Hamish Hamilton, 1964.
The New Industrial State. London, Hamish Hamilton, 1967.
Perspectives on Conservation: essays on America's natural resources. Ed. by Henry Jarrett. Homewood, Baltimore, Johns Hopkins Press, 1960.
The Scotch. Boston, Mass., Houghton Mifflin, 1964.
The Triumph; a novel of modern diplomacy. Boston, Mass., Houghton Mifflin, 1968; London, Hamish Hamilton, 1968.
Who Needs the Democrats; and what it takes to be needed. New York, Doubleday, 1970.

KAHN, HERMAN

Can We Win in Vietnam? With members of the staff of the Hudson Institute. Hudson Institute, 1969.
The Emerging Japanese Superstate; challenge and response. Englewood Cliffs, Prentice-Hall, 1970.
On Escalation; metaphors and scenarios. New York, Praeger, 1965. (Hudson Institute Series on National Security and International Order, No. 1.)
On Thermonuclear War. Princeton, N.J., Princeton University Press, 1961.
Thinking About the Unthinkable. New York, Horizon Press, 1962.
The Year 2000; a framework for speculation on the next thirty-three years. Co-authored with Anthony Wiener. New York, Macmillan; London, Collier-Macmillan, 1967.

MENDE, TIBOR

L'Amérique latine entre en scène. Paris, Editions du Seuil, 1956.
L'Asie du sud-est entre deux mondes. Paris, Editions du Seuil, 1954.
Au Pays de la mousson. Paris, Editions du Seuil, 1954.
China and Her Shadow. English translation. London, Coward-McCann, 1962.
La Chine et son ombre. Paris, Editions du Seuil, 1960.
The Chinese Revolution. London, Thames, 1961.
Conversations with Mr Nehru. London, Secker & Warburg, 1956.
Entre la peur et l'espoir. Réflexions sur l'histoire d'aujourd'hui. Paris, Editions du Seuil, 1958.
L'Inde devant l'orage. Paris, Editions du Seuil, 1951.
Regards sur l'histoire de demain. Paris, Editions du Seuil, 1954.
La Révolte de l'Asie. Paris, P.U.F., 1951.
Un Monde possible. French translation by Magdeleine Paz. Paris, Editions du Seuil, 1963.

PERLMUTTER, HOWARD V.

Towards a Theory and Practice of Social Architecture; the building of indispensable institutions. London, Tavistock, 1965.

INDEX

Africa: finance, 88
agriculture: farm products, 24, 90–1;
    food, 66
aid, foreign, 64–7, 95
Aitken, Thomas, 12
America, Latin: economics, 68–74;
    finance and investment, 72ff, 88;
    food, 70; GNP, 71–2; labour, 70–1;
    military regimes, 75–6; nationalism,
    76–7; population, urban, 54, 66, 68–
    72; socio-political problems, 75–6;
    tariffs, 80–1; trade, 73–4 (regional
    integration), 71–2, 78–81
Amstutz, Arnold E., 134–43, 159
Andean Common Market, 71–2, 78, 80
Ansoff, H. Igor, 124–33, 159
Asia: balance of power, 49; economics,
    50; food, 54; GNP, 54–5; Japanese
    economic aid, 50–1; regional co-
    operation, 52–3
Asian Development Bank, 53
Asian Industrial Development Coun-
    cil, 53
Association of Southeast Asian
    Nations, 53
Australia: economics, 59–60; Japanese
    trade rivalry, 51, 60; New Zealand
    trade, 53–4; Pacific development, 53

Bretton Woods, 84
Business International S.A., 12, 89, 97

Canada: economy, 40–1; GNP, 41;
    market, 40–1
Central American Common Market,
    71, 79–81
Centre d'Études Industrielles, 12, 155
China: cultural revolution, 62–3;
    economics, 50, 60–4; GNP, 60–1; and

lesser developed countries, 66–7;
    trade, 62–4
computers: marketing information
    uses, 134–43
corporations: corporative strategy,
    124–33; marketing information
    systems (computerized), 134–43;
    'megafirms' and types of firms, 113–
    23; see also management; monetary
    systems, international
Curzon, Gerard, 31–4, 91

Drucker, Peter F., 128

Eurobonds, 104–6
Eurodollar, 23, 25, 97–8, 102–3, 106
Europe: consumer expenditure, 19;
    corporate mergers, 18–19, 24; cor-
    porate opportunities in, 15–16, 24–5,
    29–30, 35–7; defence, 21; economy,
    16–24, 28; finance and currency, 23,
    25, 33–4, 84–7, 97–8, 102–3; GNP, 16;
    international companies, 17–18;
    labour, 21–3, 25; management, role
    of, 28–30; markets and marketing,
    16–20, 24–5; medical costs, 20;
    monetary union, 33–4; national
    governments, 15; nationalism, 26–7;
    politics, 16, 21, 27–30; R & D, 18;
    retail trade, 20–1, 25; sales costs, 20;
    tariffs, 15; technology, 18; trade and
    industry, 17; unification of, 15–18,
    22–34; US investment in, 19, 24, 38
Europe, East, 21–3
European Economic Community:
    corporate mergers, 18; EFTA trade
    91; French attitude to, 32–3
    membership, 33 91–2; prices, 18,
    32; tariffs 31

161